MICROWAVE
MEALS

Published in 2024 by Hardie Grant Books,
an imprint of Hardie Grant Publishing

Hardie Grant Books (London)
5th & 6th Floors
52–54 Southwark Street
London SE1 1UN

Hardie Grant Books (Melbourne)
Building 1, 658 Church Street
Richmond, Victoria 3121

hardiegrantbooks.com

British Library Cataloguing-in-Publication
Data. A catalogue record for this book
is available from the British Library.

Microwave Meals
ISBN: 978-1-78488-708-7

10 9 8 7 6 5 4 3 2 1

Publishing Director: Kajal Mistry
Senior Editor: Eila Purvis
Design and Art Direction: Evi-O.Studio |
Emi Chiba & Matthew Crawford
Photographer: Sam A Harris
Food stylist: Tamara Vos
Prop stylist: Rachel Vere
Recipe tester: Sarah Geraghty
Copy-editor: Esme Curtis
Proofreader: Kathy Steer
Production Controller: Sabeena Atchia

Colour reproduction by p2d
Printed and bound in China by
Leo Paper Products Ltd.

DELICIOUS RECIPES TO SAVE TIME, EFFORT AND ENERGY

TIM ANDERSON
MICROWAVE MEALS

PHOTOGRAPHY
BY SAM A. HARRIS

Hardie Grant
BOOKS

MAINS
84

SWEETS
134

A MICROWAVE MANIFESTO

We are the microwavers: the open-minded optimists who embrace technology, excited by its potential to make our lives easier and our meals more delicious. Many of us are also, it must be said, short on time, energy and funds. The microwave can help us mitigate all of these issues.

It's obvious that the microwave has the capacity to expedite our cooking. What may be less obvious is it may also improve the quality of our lives. The microwave can save effort, energy, time and money, in small but not trivial ways. The microwave is a tool for cooking, but it can also be a tool for alleviating stress and anxiety, for nourishment that goes beyond nutrition.

Put it this way: you can make a risotto the old-fashioned way, ladling stock, stirring, ladling stock, stirring, ladling stock, stirring, ladling stock, stirring, ladling stock, stirring, until it's finally done, and by that time your kids are all grown up and have left the house and your dog is dead and you realise you missed out on so much because you were too busy ladling stock and stirring *forever*.

With the microwave, this needn't be the case. You can put the risotto in the microwave for 8 minutes, then go and dance with your family to a couple of Taylor Swift songs, come back to stir it up, pop it back in for another 8 minutes, then go and dance some more. Or you can use those 8 minutes to do part of a Joe Wicks video, or build something, or have a cup of tea, or do yoga, or help your kids with their homework, or drink an ice-cold Kinnie in the sunshine. Let the microwave take care of dinner, so you can take care of yourself.

MY MICROWAVE AND ME

For years, I didn't have a microwave. Didn't need one, didn't want one. What were they good for, anyway, besides reheating lasagne and maybe popping the occasional bag of popcorn? But at some point, my mother-in-law gave us her old microwave when she had her kitchen redone. My initial attitude towards it was a mix of annoyance at the amount of counter space it took up, and gratitude that I no longer had to wash up a pan whenever I needed to warm up leftover takeaways.

But for the most part, I was indifferent. I didn't think of it as an actual tool for cooking until I started to find surprising, creative uses for it. And, like so many things in my life I feel grateful for, I have Japan to thank for opening my eyes to the countless possibilities of microwave cookery.

THE JAPAN CONNECTION

Some of you may already be familiar with me as an author of Japanese cookbooks. Very long story short: I've been interested in Japanese food from when I was about 15 years old. I went on to study it in college, lived in Japan for a couple years and ultimately wound up cooking and writing about Japanese food professionally after winning *MasterChef* in 2011. As a chef and restaurateur, I specialised in ramen – an exceedingly complex and difficult dish – but I have actually always gravitated towards simple Japanese home cooking that utilises strong seasonings and speedy techniques to make very delicious food with little effort.

I already knew that because Japanese kitchens are often quite short on space, small cooking appliances like microwaves, rice cookers, toaster ovens and electric hot plates are put to good use to make the most of limited set-ups. But I didn't realise just how versatile microwaves are until I began following Japanese Instagram accounts that focused on quick and easy recipes, and soon noticed that many of them use the microwave to expedite prep, or even make complete dishes, as a matter of routine. They were used for everything, from basics to surprising tricks like cooking spaghetti in so little water it doesn't even require draining. As a time-poor (and inherently lazy) working parent I was excited by the microwave's potential for facilitating good, nourishing meals. I soon began using it every day.

But even though it was Japan that introduced me to the wonders of microwave cooking, this isn't a Japanese cookbook. There are a few Japanese or Japanese-influenced dishes, but generally the recipes are a real mix of things. This is deliberate. I have tried to choose a wide range of dishes in order to showcase the versatility of microwave cooking, and to cover a multitude of useful techniques. My goal is to present you with methods and ideas that you can then apply to your own style of cooking. For example, if you can learn the basics of cooking risotto in the microwave (page 86), you can then change that recipe up with whatever ingredients or seasonings you like. The same goes for making pasta, cakes, sauces, curries, custards – you name it! The fun thing about microwaving is finding ways that it can help you make the food you already love to cook. Think of it as your little sous chef. You just have to get to know it.

YOUR MICROWAVE AND YOU: READ THIS FIRST!

I assume you already own a microwave. (If not: get one!) But what I can't assume is what you use that microwave for, or more importantly, what you *want* to use it for. Regardless of your specific microwave goals, I hope this book can help you achieve them. But I can only guide you so far; to become a microwave maestro, you have to use your own experience and instincts, just like you would with any kind of cooking.

HOW TO MICROWAVE

I'm often guilty of skipping over the introductory sections in cookbooks, especially when I think I've already got a handle on the given style of cookery. *Come on, let's get to the recipes already!* But please, if you are like me, I am asking you sincerely to read all of this, even if you're pretty confident with microwave cooking already. There are some important bits here that not only will help you develop microwave know-how generally, but also information that clarifies specific things about the recipes.

PROCEED WITH CAUTION! AND BE PREPARED TO IMPROVISE

What works for me, in my microwave, may not yield quite the same results for others. In some cases this is a matter of correcting for different wattages, but that's just one of many variables that can change the outcome of your cooking. These variables include the starting temperature of the ingredients, the density and water content of those ingredients, and what kind of containers you use. Since all of these alter cook times and heat distribution, any microwave recipes should only be taken as a guide, and you will likely have to make adjustments as you cook.

Frankly, it pains me as a professional cookery writer to tell you that these recipes are not foolproof, but they're not. No microwave recipes are! But I am certain you can make the recipes work for you, with a little improvisation and fine-tuning.

The first rule of thumb when approaching microwave cooking is to err on the side of caution, with lower cook times and possibly lower power levels, if you have a really strong microwave. I tested these recipes in an 800W microwave – which is among the more common wattages people buy, though a lot of people have a 900W machine. Less common are 700W microwaves and ones that are 1000W or more. There is a conversion chart for cook times and power levels on page 22, but regardless of your power level, when you cook a new recipe it is wise to check on the food as it cooks. This is particularly true when cooking small volumes, which absorb the full blast of your microwave's output (as opposed to large volumes, which only absorb radiation down to a certain depth), so the heating power becomes much faster and more intense.

To give an example: if a recipe says to heat a knob of butter for 30 seconds to melt it, the first time around I would check it after 15 seconds just to see how it's getting on, regardless of your microwave wattage. This will allow you to make adjustments on the fly. Maybe you've got a 700W machine, so 30 seconds seems short – but what if you're using a container that turns out to be particularly conductive? Or what if your butter has a slightly higher water content than another brand you've used before, causing it to heat up faster? Or maybe you keep the butter in a warmer part of the refrigerator, which will make it take less time to melt? Many, many things can alter how things behave in the microwave – so take it slow at first, pausing often to check, observe, learn and adjust.

BUT ALSO: DON'T IMPROVISE!

While I generally recommend taking a curious, independent approach to microwave cooking to find out what works best for you, there are certain situations in which you should not deviate from what I've written. I flag these instances in specific recipes wherever it's really important, mainly with regards to what kind of container and/or cover to use. I have tried to make these recipes as user-friendly as possible, and I don't want to tell people they have to go out and buy specific containers or crockery to make the recipes work. But in some cases, these things do matter.

Similarly, as a general rule I also advise against ingredient substitutions, but mainly because I haven't tested them and I'm not sure how they'll behave. Certain foods that are really quite similar to the ingredients list will work, of course, but I'm talking swapping out minced (ground) pork for minced turkey, or frozen peas for frozen corn, that sort of thing.

And this is the fun flipside of cooking in the microwave with an inquisitive mind: once you understand how different things cook, you can build on that knowledge and try new things.

MICROWAVE HEATING BASICS

Microwaves work by blasting food with electromagnetic radiation. That might sound scary, but it's not quite the same kind of radiation you get from, say, plutonium. Of course, it should be obvious from their effects on food that microwaves would *absolutely* mess you up if you had the extraordinary bad luck of being exposed directly to them, but safely locked away inside their little metal boxes, they don't cause people to get sick or cells to mutate the way more hardcore forms of radiation do. As far as I'm concerned, microwaving is one of the safer methods of cooking (more on this in Microwave Safety, page 25, and Why to Microwave, page 26), and this is largely because the heat is so focused and contained.

Microwaves are able to rapidly agitate molecules, which increases their kinetic energy and causes them to heat up. This works on carbohydrates, proteins, sugars – pretty much everything food is made of – but it is especially good at heating up water and fat. This has some very cool, very useful effects on food. Perhaps at its most basic, microwave cooking is akin to steaming or boiling, but without the need for excess water. Most foods, especially vegetables, are mostly water anyway, so they can be steamed from within using their own moisture. You can also, of course, add varying levels of water to the cooking vessel. A small amount will simply assist with the steaming process and help prevent the food from drying out or scorching; a large amount will become a medium for boiling. This means that the usefulness of water-based microwave cooking doesn't stop at steaming greens. You can use it to cook rice, pasta, pulses (legumes), fish, eggs, even certain meats – anything, really, that could be done by boiling, poaching or simmering.

Microwaves' ability to heat fat is similarly useful. While it takes a little longer to get going than water, it actually gets much hotter. Using fat as a medium for cooking in the microwave creates an effect similar to frying, rapidly softening and even browning foods. This can be really useful, for everything from making curries (page 94) to infusing oils (page 33) to cooking bacon (page 34) to toasting nuts (page 141). But be warned: because oil can get *so* hot in the microwave, it can burn food, burn you and also damage containers (see more on cooking vessels – opposite).

Microwave cooking often has a reputation for being uneven or unpredictable, and we've all had that annoying experience of trying to defrost or cook something from frozen, only to find that it winds up with spots that are rocket-hot and others that are still icy. In this particular instance, microwave radiation penetrates beneath the surface of the food and heats water or fat molecules within it, while 'missing' other parts of the dish where the water remains locked within its frozen crystalline structure. So while microwaves may seem inconsistent, it's only because they generate heat in a way that doesn't feel intuitive compared to directional heat sources such as a gas flame or a grill (broiler). But once the fat or water at any position within a dish reaches boiling temperature (or higher), it will quickly pass that heat onto the rest of the dish. When we conceptualise the microwave as simply a different means for boiling, steaming or frying foods, it becomes easier to understand how they are able to do unexpected things like cooking pasta or browning garlic.

On the topic of even heating, the recipes and methods in this book assume the presence of a turntable, which are standard on most (but not all) machines. If your microwave does not have a turntable, you will have to manually rotate the food periodically throughout cooking.

COOKING VESSELS

Of course, the food itself is only part of the equation when it comes to understanding how heat works in the microwave. This is because different materials absorb, reflect and retain heat from the microwave radiation and/or from the food itself as it heats. This is another part of microwave cooking that can make it feel unpredictable, and it's another situation where you'll have to use your own experience to figure out what works best – the 'microwave safe' label applied to so many containers doesn't mean they'll provide good results, and in fact some of them aren't even that safe! I have these particular 'microwave-safe' red ceramic bowls at home that I know at this point to never put in the microwave – not because they melt or spark or release chemicals or anything like that, but because they become *insanely* hot, even while the food itself isn't that warm. I guess this is because the bowls themselves are too conductive when it comes to microwave radiation? I don't know. But whatever the reason, no way are they 'microwave safe'! I hate those red bowls.

THE MICROWAVE BLACKLIST

Demonic red bowls aside, there are a few obvious materials that are categorically NOT microwave safe, so let's get those out of the way first:

Weirdly, although we're always told that metal is a big no-no, technically you can put it in the microwave – and indeed, microwaves' internal casings are made of metal. This is because flat, smooth pieces of metal simply reflect the radiation, so the walls of the oven make it bounce around and (theoretically) enable more omnidirectional and therefore more even cooking. Some of my old microwave cookbooks recommend using sheets of foil to protect the surface of foods from drying out for a similar reason, and even some dedicated microwave cookware has metal elements because it doesn't absorb microwave energy and therefore stays relatively cool.

But – and this is a huge but – only metal that is perfectly smooth and flat should go in the microwave, and I personally wouldn't even do that, just out of an abundance of caution. All my life I've been told that metal + microwaves = bad news. This is because metal that has any irregular or protruding parts, such as a crinkly surface on foil or the tines of a fork, can cause electrical arcing, and that's how you end up with your microwave on fire. Don't do it.

As for melamine: it's not meant to be microwave-safe anyway, and the reason for that is obvious if you've ever made the mistake of heating it in the microwave. Best-case scenario is it becomes finger-blisteringly hot even during a short cook. Worst case scenario is it shatters, melts or scorches. Not only that, but melamine can expel seriously dangerous chemicals when microwaved – and this is where we come to bamboo fibre. While pure bamboo fibre crockery would simply warp in the microwave, a lot of it is actually mixed with melamine as a binding agent.

As for non-microwaveable plastics, they could melt or leach potentially harmful chemicals into your food. Among these chemicals is the fairly frightening BPA, which can mess with your hormones and endocrine functions. This is already banned in the production of baby bottles, but make sure any plastic you put in the microwave is labelled BPA-free.

THE 'GREY AREA' MATERIALS

In addition to the materials above that you definitely shouldn't put in the microwave, there are a few that are kinda-sorta okay, but kinda-sorta not, and I tend to avoid them if I can. These are:

'MICROWAVE-SAFE' PLASTICS

CERAMICS

Now, you may be thinking: wuh? Of course microwave-safe plastics and ceramics are microwave safe. But I have reasons!

Plastics can be labelled 'microwave safe' when the material itself is robust against microwave radiation, but this doesn't mean it can't be damaged by the heat of the food if it reaches very high temperatures. Fat and sugar can both get way hotter than the boiling point of water, and this is where plastics tend to fail. I have some so-called 'microwave-safe' plastic containers at home with some gnarly microwave battle scars, and these came from mundane jobs like reheating curry and melting butter. So as a general rule, I tend to avoid plastics in the microwave – but not always. In fact, the low conductivity of plastics make them ideal for certain things, like baking cakes without them getting too hot along the edges (see pages 140–151 for recipes).

Ceramics, while generally safe, can also be a bit all over the place. Most of them are absolutely fine. But some of them are made with minerals that are conductive to microwave radiation and can become crazily hot – as in the evil red bowls I mentioned on the previous page. In my kitchen, I know which ceramic dishes are benign, and which ones will burn my hands down to smouldering stumps, like a couple of blown-out matches. You'll have to figure out which ones work for you because, unfortunately, all ceramics are a bit different. But one obvious thing to avoid would be any dishes with metallic glazes or inlays.

THE PRIZE WINNERS

This leaves us with two materials that I generally prefer above all others for microwave cooking, and they are:

GLASS
(microwave-safe, of course)

SILICONE

When I cook in the microwave, I almost always reach for the same cooking vessel: my trusty 3 litre (101 fl oz/12 cup) borosilicate glass bowl. I prefer glass for a number of reasons: I don't have to worry about it leaking chemicals, melting or being damaged by high temperatures; it doesn't retain smells; it allows microwaves to pass through freely, so they can more rapidly heat the food; and it conducts and redistributes heat in a way that encourages even cooking, but not in a way that gets so terrifyingly hot that I feel like I have to use a pair of crucible tongs to handle it. It is, for the vast majority of microwave cooking jobs, perfect.

Size is an important factor in my preference for this particular container, too. I usually use the 3 litre (101 fl oz/12 cup) bowl even for smaller quantities of food, as the deeper walls help naturally mitigate spattering and overboiling. I love my big glass bowl!

As for silicone, there are some very strong pros as well: it isn't very conductive, it won't be damaged by either radiation or high food temperatures, and it's (kind of) non-stick. These make it ideal for dense items like brownie batter (page 138) that require even heat distribution to prevent them from being overdone on the outside and underdone in the middle. It has one major con, however: it's floppy. This can make it difficult to handle, and annoying to clean. Still, for certain things, especially baked goods, it's one of my favourite materials to microwave.

COVERING TECHNIQUES

Throughout this book, I use two terms: 'cover' and 'cover loosely'. Before I describe what I mean by those, I should note that you should basically never cover food *tightly* in the microwave – there should always be some way of venting steam and pressure, especially with prolonged cooks. I have some containers with little holes built into their lids specifically for ventilation, and even these have blown off when the pressure builds up too much. Always make sure your lids are not tightly sealed to avoid this.

When I say 'cover', I mean the cooking vessel should be covered, but still in a way that allows for excess steam to escape. I usually do this with a plate (microwave safe, obvs) that fits nicely over my container – usually my favourite 3 litre (101 fl oz/12 cup) glass bowl. The plate is heavy enough to keep most of the steam inside the bowl, but the lack of a seal means the container never becomes pressurised.

When I say 'cover loosely', it means that the plate or lid should be placed at a jaunty angle over the top of the bowl, to the extent that there's a significant gap for steam to escape. In these cases, the cover is there mainly to prevent splattering and not to retain steam or circulate heat. Now, I should say that using a plate (or lid or whatever) is not actually my preferred method of covering food. I prefer to use cling film (plastic wrap), which is the norm in Japanese microwave cookery.

Cling film has a few key advantages over any other kind of cover. First of all, it can create a tight seal while also stretching to accommodate excess steam pressure. When it comes to covering 'loosely', it's also a winner because you can literally just drape it haphazardly over any container like a duvet on a badly made bed. You can also cover a container tightly with cling film, then poke holes in the top of it to allow steam to escape while still minimising splatter.

BUT! Even though I really like how cling film performs in the microwave, I don't use it that much any more, for a few reasons. First of all, if you have to un-cover and then re-cover food, it's really annoying. Usually the cling film tears or warps, and can't be re-used, so you have to tear off a new piece to re-cover. And this brings us to the biggest problem with cling film: it's a single-use plastic that can't be recycled, and that's no good at all, especially if one of the reasons you're using the microwave is to try and lessen your environmental impact.

The main thing here is to mind whether instructions say 'cover' or 'cover loosely', and understand what those things mean. What you use for the cover itself is up to you.

STARTING TEMPERATURES

The recipes in this book assume 'normal' starting temperatures of room temperature or colder, but not frozen, unless specified. For example, when a recipe calls for water, this should be just cold water from the tap – not hot water, and certainly not boiling.

Similarly, if a recipe calls for something that's usually refrigerated, then I assume those things will be cooked from refrigerator temperature. In the case of eggs, I keep mine in the refrigerator (they honestly do last longer in there), but if you keep yours at room temperature, consider reducing the cook time on egg-based recipes slightly. When a recipe calls for frozen anything – frozen peas, frozen dumplings, etc. – then those should go in frozen, unless I specify that they should be defrosted first.

USEFUL KIT

I've written this book assuming that the microwave is literally the only cooking appliance you have. No hob, no oven, no toaster, not even a kettle. Likewise, there's no electrical prep machinery required here – no blenders, food processors, mixers, whatever. And you won't need any microwave-specific cookware, either – most of that stuff is a borderline-useless scam anyway. But you will need some basic stuff!

A variety of microwave-safe cooking vessels in a range of shapes and sizes, especially glass bowls, but also plastic bowls and containers, and glass or ceramic baking dishes. Silicone is also very useful for particular recipes, which I have noted in the recipes themselves.

Scales, measuring cups, measuring jugs and measuring spoons.
Not all of the measurements in this book need to be totally precise, but it should go without saying that if your measurements are way off, then the recipes just won't work. With microwave cooking, you can't rely on your senses and intuition to change things on the fly as much as you can with more hands-on methods, so accuracy is important.

Oven gloves: not totally necessary but a lot more reliable than an awkwardly folded dish towel! Cooking vessels can get really hot in the microwave, so these are a good investment if you don't have some already.

Basic food prep stuff: knives, graters, sieves (fine mesh strainers), whisks, spoons, spatulas, etc. A good flexible spatula is particularly useful for stirring stuff up and scraping down the sides of containers.

SCALING

One major drawback of microwave cooking is that recipes don't scale well because cooking times depend not only on the volume of food but also its density and macronutrient make-up (and many other factors). Of course, you *can* scale things, up or down, but if you do, you'll have to do your own experimenting with cooking times, and frankly, you're on your own! Remember: *proceed with caution and be prepared to improvise.*

Serving sizes provided here are generally quite generous. Too little? Make another dish! Or just have some crusty bread handy. And if the serving size is too big, then just have the rest as leftovers. After all: you've got a microwave! So reheating them is not a challenge.

WATTAGE CONVERSTIONS AND POWER LEVELS

All of the recipes in this book are written for an 800W microwave. But obviously not everyone has an 800W machine; common wattages range from 600 to 1000. Below you will find a conversion chart to get the right cook time for your microwave, but actually, you don't really need it. You just need to remember some simple multipliers:

For 600W	multiply cook times (in seconds) by 1.3
For 700W	multiply by 1.1
For 900W	multiply by 0.9
For 100W	multiply by 0.8

For any other microwave power, the multiplier is simply 800 divided by whatever wattage you have. So, for example, if a recipe calls for a cook time of 3 minutes, then for a 1200W microwave it would be 800 ÷ 1200 × 180 = 120 seconds, or 2 minutes.

For simplicity, in the following table I've rounded all timings to the nearest 5 seconds.

600W	700W	800W (recipe default)	900W	1000W
0:20	0:20	**0:15**	0:15	0:10
0:40	0:35	**0:30**	0:25	0:25
1:20	1:10	**1:00**	0:55	0:50
2:00	1:40	**1:30**	1:20	1:10
2:40	2:20	**2:00**	1:45	1:35
3:20	2:50	**2:30**	2:15	2:00
4:00	3:25	**3:00**	2:40	2:25
4:40	4:00	**3:30**	3:05	2:50
5:20	4:35	**4:00**	3:35	3:10
6:00	5:10	**4:30**	4:00	3:35
6:40	5:40	**5:00**	4:25	4:00
8:00	6:50	**6:00**	5:20	4:50
9:20	8:00	**7:00**	6:15	5:35
10:40	9:10	**8:00**	7:05	6:25
12:00	10:15	**9:00**	8:00	7:10
13:20	11:25	**10:00**	8:55	8:00
16:00	13:40	**12:00**	10:40	9:35
20:00	17:10	**15:00**	13:20	12:00
26:40	22:50	**20:00**	17:45	16:00
40:00	34:20	**30:00**	26:40	24:00

Remember: these timings, like all microwave cooking times, should be taken as a guide, not as gospel. Many other factors determine cook time besides just wattage. Use your best judgement and always check on your food, especially when trying a new dish. On that note, remember that you can always cook something longer if it's undercooked – but overcooked food is not salvageable.

Some recipes require using different power levels, which on my microwave, can be inputted on a scale from one to ten. Frustratingly, I have no idea what these power levels actually do. Obviously they lower the output power – but by how much? Nobody knows. It's very annoying, and because most microwaves are like this, it makes providing accurate conversions impossible. More annoying still is the fact that some microwaves simply provide power levels as high, medium-high, medium, etc., rather than as numbers.

But as a very, very rough conversion guide, if your microwave is lower than 800W, bump the power up one level for each 100W difference, and if your microwave is higher than 800W, bump the power down one level. So, for example, if a recipe calls for power level 6, on a 600W microwave you should actually use power level 8; on a 900W machine you should use power level 5. There's no need to adjust power levels unless the recipe indicates it – everything else can just be cooked at full power, regardless of your microwave's maximum wattage – bearing in mind the adjusted cook times outlined above.

Again, I must reiterate that this is only a loose guide – use common sense and a bit of caution and remember to check and observe as you go.

BROWNING IS OVERRATED

OR: HOW I LEARNED TO STOP WORRYING AND LOVE SEASONING

So often when I tell people I'm writing a microwave cookbook, the response is incredulous. A lot of people seem to think that microwaving is simply an inferior cooking method, and a particularly common refrain from microwave naysayers is: but what about BROWNING?!?

As if BROWNING is the only way to make food taste good. Don't get me wrong: browning is nice. The burnished surface of a puff pastry pie lid, the sear on a steak and the rich sweetness of sautéed shallots – all of this is the stuff of browning, and we are told, so often, that *this* is the key to delicious food.

Well, let me offer a counterpoint: browning is for losers who don't understand how to season their food. Okay, yes, fine, browning is desirable, even irreplaceable, in some situations. If you served me an un-browned steak (for example), I would take it as an act of deliberate antagonism and provocation. But it just isn't necessary for many foods – maybe not even most foods – to make them taste good. And this brings us back to the Japan connection (page 8).

A lot of Japanese cooking doesn't rely on browning for deliciousness. Sushi is an obvious one. Hotpots such as shabu-shabu are another. Then there is the whole world of *nimono* – simmered dishes – which use umami-rich broths to enhance the natural flavours of good produce. And of course, ramen – one of the world's most beloved foods – is made mostly by boiling bones, without browning them first. All manner of Japanese microwave recipes simply don't even consider browning, because cuisine often achieves deliciousness in so many other ways, mainly through seasonings. Key among these are miso and soy sauce which provide umami, salt, aroma and depth.

But seasonings like this are not unique to Japan, nor to East Asia generally. Every culture has ingredients used to deliver umami and caramelised or Maillard (i.e. 'browning') flavours. To name a few from British cuisine specifically, we have Worcestershire sauce, Marmite, brown sugar, bacon and mature cheese, all of which lend a deep, satisfying savouriness to food. Elsewhere in Europe, we have olives, anchovies, tomatoes, red wine, fermented vegetables ... and more cheese!

You will therefore find these kinds of ingredients used throughout the book, among other flavour enhancers. The great cookery writer and presenter Andi Oliver once complained about the (mis)use of the word 'seasoning', annoyed at how it has been reduced to mean just adding salt, and maybe pepper, to foods. In Andi's view, seasoning should be *seasoning* – using all of the tools in the shed, all of the spices in the cabinet, to enhance your food. I am fully on board with this. With things like chilli, garam masala, smoked paprika and any number of fresh or dried herbs at our disposal – seriously, who needs browning?

MICROWAVE SAFETY!

Generally speaking, microwave cooking is very safe. I admit that microwave radiation itself is a little scary, but as long as you don't mess around with your microwave, or attempt to use it after it's been damaged, these do not pose any danger. But there are a few potential hazards to note.

First of all is the risk of fire if you put the wrong material in the microwave – see page 14 for details. A related risk is chemical leakage from certain materials; be mindful that even so-called 'microwave-safe' plastics can still expel weird chemicals into your food. Make sure you use containers that are BPA-free, at the very least.

Another potential danger in microwave cookery is undercooked food. Of course, that goes for any kind of cooking, but in the microwave it's a little bit harder to gauge doneness using your senses, especially because heat distribution can be uneven. Always check that high-risk foods like chicken or fish are cooked through before serving, and if they're not, whack 'em back in for a minute or two.

Beyond that, the main risks of microwave cooking come from scalding and burning. In particular, be very careful when you remove the lid or cling film (plastic wrap) from a container – the steam can come billowing out with surprising force and fierce heat. When handling any container that comes out of the microwave, use a thick dish towel or, better yet, oven gloves, which offer more protection and a better grip.

One final thing to note is that food can boil dry in the microwave, even though there's no direct heat source. If there's insufficient water in a dish, food can burn and containers (mainly plastic ones) can be damaged. So always check on your food during cooking to see if it's drying out, especially if it's something you've not cooked before or if it's a particularly long cook time.

WHY TO MICROWAVE

We've covered the how-to of microwaving; what about the why-to? Here are some of the main reasons I love to microwave:

SAVE TIME

Microwave cooking isn't always the faster option, but sometimes it certainly is, both in terms of the overall cook time and the hands-on time.

SAVE ENERGY (AND POSSIBLY MONEY)

Microwaving is one of the most energy-efficient ways to cook, because heat is transferred directly into the food, and because the machines themselves consume less energy to run than a hob or an oven. However, if you're looking to save money on bills, and you have a gas cooker, that still might be the cheaper option, depending on the fuel rates at any given time. But as a general rule, if there's something that you could cook in the microwave instead of a different electric appliance, then you probably should – it's usually more economical.

SAVE WATER

For jobs like steaming vegetables or boiling pasta, you can use a lot less water than you would if you cooked them on the hob. In fact, with some veg you don't need to add any water at all.

SAVE THE ENVIRONMENT (SORT OF)

Alright, you're not going to reverse global warming by using your microwave every day. But by saving energy and water, you're at least doing a little bit!

SAVE SPACE

Think of the microwave as just another cooker, which you can utilise to free up hob space, oven space, etc. when you're cooking multiple things. This is especially useful when you're preparing something relatively complex, like Christmas dinner – just whack the sprouts in the microwave! You can even cook them in their serving dish, which brings us to ...

SAVE WASHING UP

Sometimes, microwaving makes the washing up easier. This is primarily because you can cook in serving dishes or storage containers, but also because sometimes microwave cooking eliminates the need for additional pots and pans. Making risotto, for example, doesn't require an additional pan for the stock, and you can even cook pasta together with its sauce in the same bowl. Plus, what you do wash up tends to be easier than if it had come from the oven or the hob, because food doesn't stick to the cookware as much. Advantage: microwave!

SAVE EFFORT

Washing up is just one way the microwave helps lighten the kitchen load. Mainly, it reduces the need for hands-on cooking because the food requires less stirring and turning, since the heat is omnidirectional and less prone to sticking or scorching.

REDUCE HAZARDS (ESPECIALLY WITH KIDS)

I have a one year old and a five year old, both of whom are very curious about what goes on in the kitchen, but have absolutely no sense of danger. This means I'm constantly on edge about them being in the kitchen. One of the worst things that could happen would be knocking a hot pan off of the hob, and onto themselves. Yikes. Cooking in the microwave completely eliminates this risk and other similar dangers.

REDUCE MESS

My hob has been unimaginably clean since I started testing recipes for this book. Sure, you have to clean the microwave from time to time. But generally speaking, it's an incredibly low-mess means of cooking.

PRESERVE FLAVOUR AND NUTRIENTS

I don't know if this is actually true, but I've heard that because microwaves agitate certain molecules but not others, they're good at preserving both flavour compounds and nutrients. I'm not going to say microwaving will make you healthier, because it probably (definitely) won't. But like ... maybe it will???

MAKE YOUR MICROWAVE WORK FOR YOU

While most of the recipes in this book are quite fast and simple – which is the whole point, really – a few of them are a bit more complicated and time-consuming. I've included these to illustrate just how much a microwave can do, and they can be broken down into much simpler constituent parts that may be more useful to you than the recipes in their entirety. For example, the creme patissiere with citrus curd (page 137) will show you how to make both the custard and the curd, which you can then use in other dishes or simply on their own. Similarly, the meatball subs (page 118) contain a classic Italian-American red sauce, which can be enjoyed on pasta on its own. Feel free to find ways to make the recipes work for you.

BAS

ICS

STOCK

Amazingly, you can make a pretty decent stock in the microwave. This works with vegetables and smaller bones, i.e. chicken or fish, perhaps pork ribs – but not big chunky ones like beef ribs or lamb shanks. The bones should be pre-cooked, but this is mainly to keep the broth from getting scummy.

Pile the bones into a large bowl and add whatever veg you like – onions and their skins, leeks, celery, garlic, ginger, etc. – then add enough water to cover. Cover the bowl and cook for 20–30 minutes.

Ladle the broth through a sieve (fine mesh strainer) and keep in the refrigerator for up to 5 days, or in the freezer for up to 6 months. Note that this method tends to render quite a lot of fat. You can either just keep the fat together with the broth (it's delicious and rich), or you can carefully remove the fat from the surface once the broth is chilled, to be used for something else.

PASTA

Pasta in the microwave is very cool because it cooks in so little water, and you can start it cooking in cold water. For larger quantities, this makes the total cook time a little longer than conventional boiling, but actually, when you take into consideration the time it takes to boil the water in the first place, it's about the same.

To do this, place the pasta in a bowl and add water, a little bit of oil and some salt. Cover loosely and cook on full power, for these recommended times, stirring once halfway through cooking:

PASTA WEIGHT	WATER VOLUME	TIME
100 g (3½ oz)	220 ml (7½ fl oz/scant 1 cup)	8–10 minutes
200 g (7 oz)	440 ml (15 fl oz/scant 2 cups)	12–14 minutes
300 g (10½ oz)	660 ml (22 fl oz/2¾ cups)	16–18 minutes

TIP   I wouldn't cook more than 300 g (10½ oz) in the microwave – at that point it isn't any more efficient than doing it on the hob. When the pasta is done, it will have a little bit of very starchy water left – this can be discarded, or used as the foundation of a sauce (see recipes, pages 66 and 112).

NOTE   You can also cook pasta and sauce together in the same bowl, as in the Rigatoni alla Gin Martini on page 128. However, you will still need the indicated amount of water, so the total volume of food being heated will be significantly larger and therefore the cook time will be accordingly longer. How much longer depends on many things, but for 200 g (7 oz) of pasta cooked in its sauce, I would budget at least 20 minutes in the oven. So it isn't necessarily a time-saver, but it will still save water, energy and, potentially, a bit of washing up.

RICE

Although rice doesn't actually cook any quicker in the microwave, it still has some advantages. First of all, it will never stick to the bottom of the pan – because there is no pan, and no direct heat source. Secondly, you can serve, store and reheat it in the same container it's cooked in. Yes, you can reheat rice – conventional wisdom and indeed some food labels have this wrong. Rice is perfectly safe to reheat, and does so beautifully in the microwave. The implied food safety risk isn't in the reheating, it's in the cooling and storing. If lukewarm rice is left out for too long, it can harbour a bacterium called *Bacillus cereus*, whose toxin-producing spores can cause serious illness and are not killed by reheating, even above boiling temperatures. So as long as you get your rice in the refrigerator in a reasonable amount of time (within an hour or so is absolutely fine) then there's a very, very low chance the leftovers will make you sick.

Anyway, here is my method for cooking rice. As with any recipe, the timings will vary slightly based on your microwave and your container, so check the rice towards the end of the cook time to make sure it's not drying out.

For white rice, long or short grain, any variety

300 g/360 ml (10½ oz/12 fl oz/1½ cups) rice

540 ml (18 fl oz/2¼ cups) water

Place the rice and water in a large bowl and stir. Cover tightly with cling film (plastic wrap) with holes cut in the surface, or a well-ventilated lid or plate. Cook for 10 minutes on full power. Remove bowl and stir briefly, then re-cover. Cook again for 8 minutes on power level 5. Rest, covered, for 5 more minutes.

For brown rice, any variety

300 g/360 ml (10½ oz/12 fl oz/1½ cups) brown rice

720 ml (24 fl oz/3 cups) water

Follow the same method for white rice, but cook for 25–30 minutes on full power, without stirring.

NOTE   These measurements may seem oddly specific, but that's because I base them on Japanese rice cups, which are 180 ml (6 fl oz/¾ cup) and contain two portions of rice – so 300 g/360 ml (10½ oz/12 fl oz/1½ cups) makes four servings.

POLENTA
AND PORRIDGE

Polenta, just like risotto, is wonderful in the microwave because you don't have to stand there and stir it as it cooks. It comes out evenly cooked, clump-free and surprisingly light, especially if you beat in some cream at the end (see method). The same is true of porridge (oatmeal) – no stirring, no clumping, no sticking to the pan. Just delicious wholegrain goodness in minutes.

For polenta (2 servings)

90 g (3 oz/½ cup) polenta

360 ml (12 fl oz/1½ cups) water

240 ml (8 fl oz/1 cup) milk (or more water, or stock)

salt, as needed

Combine everything in a medium bowl, stir, cover and cook for 8–9 minutes. Whisk well and season with salt before serving.

CHANGE IT UP!

After cooking, you can flavour this with cream, butter, grated cheese, garlic powder or other dry spices, sweetcorn or Boursin. I particularly like cream and Boursin in polenta; if you whisk them well they actually lighten the consistency, making it fluffy and very smooth.

For porridge (1 large or 2 small servings)

50 g (1¾ oz/½ cup) oats

240 ml (8 fl oz/1 cup) milk

Stir the oats and milk together in a bowl, cover and cook for 4 minutes. Stir again before serving.

CRISPY FRIED
SHALLOTS AND GARLIC

Amazingly, you can use the microwave to make crisp, golden shallots or garlic, a perfect garnish for so many things, from Thai salads to Danish hot dogs. (Weirdly, I have not had the same success with onions, which is puzzling to me, but hey ho.) The garlic method also yields a delicious garlic oil, ideal for drizzling over ramen or roasting potatoes.

For crispy shallots

2 banana shallots or 4 regular ones

2 tablespoons vegetable oil

Peel and halve the shallots, then slice them very, very thinly. Toss them with the oil, then spread them out in an even layer on a plate. Cook on power level 4 for 8 minutes, tossing halfway through cooking. By now the shallots should have lost most of their moisture and begun to brown. Continue to cook on power level 6 for a further 7–8 minutes, stirring them frequently, until they are richly bronzed and totally dried out.

For crispy garlic

12 garlic cloves (about 1 whole bulb), peeled and thinly sliced

vegetable oil, as needed

Place the slices of garlic in a glass or ceramic bowl with just enough vegetable oil to submerge them. Stir them up to ensure no slices are stuck to each other, then cook at full power, uncovered, for 3 minutes. At this point the garlic should be golden; stir them and keep cooking in 10-second bursts until bronze in colour. Drain on paper towels to remove any excess oil or moisture, or cool them in their oil and keep in a sealed jar.

STREAKY BACON

The internet is full of microwave techniques for crispy bacon, but the truth is none of them will ever be totally reliable for everyone. There's far too much variation in the composition of the bacon itself to have one method that works all the time. But here is how I would suggest you proceed, and then fine-tune your technique based on your own experience.

2 slices of streaky bacon

Lay the bacon out flat on a plate, not overlapping or touching, uncovered. Cook on power level 6 for 3 minutes, turning the bacon and moving it around the plate halfway through. Drape a piece of paper towel loosely over the top of the bacon to prevent splattering, then continue to cook in 30-second intervals until the bacon is crisped and browned to your liking – about 4–5 minutes total, including the initial 3 minute cook.

4 slices of streaky bacon

Lay the bacon out flat on a plate and cook, uncovered, on power level 6 for 4 minutes, turning the bacon and moving it around the plate halfway through. Drape a piece of paper towel loosely over the top of the bacon, and continue to cook in 1-minute intervals until the bacon is crisped and browned to your liking – about 6 minutes total.

6 slices of streaky bacon

The process is the same as for four slices, but it will take about 8 minutes total. Start reducing the intervals after 6 minutes.

TIP   Don't try this with back bacon! It becomes very, very dry in the microwave. This method also works much better with quite fatty bacon, and with bacon that doesn't have any added sugar.

STEAMED VEGETABLES

Even though the microwave can do all these nifty tricks, the thing I still use it for the most is simply steaming vegetables, to have as a side or the basis for a good breakfast. The following is a basic guide to cooking common vegetables, but of course, pretty much any veg you like can be microwave-steamed or -boiled, so play around with any of your favourites that aren't listed here.

Unless otherwise indicated, all of these should be cooked loosely covered. Added water, if needed, should be just a splash – about 2–3 tablespoons. As a general rule, veg should be tossed or stirred halfway through cooking for best results. Discard any excess water from the container before seasoning and serving.

VEG	SIZE (APPROX.)	PREP	ADD WATER?	TIME (APPROX.)
Asparagus	250 g (9 oz)	Trimmed or peeled, whole or cut into batons	No	2:00–2:30
Aubergines (eggplants)	250 g (9 oz, 1 medium)	Quartered and wrapped in cling film (plastic wrap)	No	4:00–6:00
Baby corn	200 g (7 oz)	Washed	Yes	3:00
Bean sprouts	300 g (10½ oz)	Washed	No	3:30–4:00
Beetroot (beet)	250 g (9 oz)	Washed or peeled	Yes	12:00
Broccoli	300 g (10½ oz)	Cut into florets; stem thinly sliced	Yes	3:00–5:00
Cabbage (Chinese/napa)	250 g (9 oz)	Roughly chopped	No	4:00
Cabbage (sweetheart/ pointed/hispi)	350 g (12 oz)	Roughly chopped	Yes	5:00
Carrots	300 g (10½ oz)	Peeled and cut into rounds	Yes	5:00
Cauliflower	400 g (14 oz, 1 medium head)	Cut into florets	Yes	6:00

VEG	SIZE (APPROX.)	PREP	ADD WATER?	TIME (APPROX.)
Daikon	150 g (5½ oz)	Peeled and sliced	Yes	3:00
Green beans	150 g (5½ oz)	Trimmed	Yes	3:30–4:30
Kale	200 g (7 oz)	Washed, de-stemmed, chopped	Yes	5:00–6:00
Leeks	200 g (7 oz, 2 medium)	Trimmed, washed and thinly sliced	No	10:00
Mangetout (snow peas)	150 g (5½ oz)	Trimmed	No	2:00
Okra	150 g (5½ oz)	De-stemmed	No	2:30
Pak choi (bok choi)	250 g (9 oz)	Quartered	No	3:00–4:00
Peas (frozen)	200 g (7 oz)	None	Yes	3:30
Pea shoots	150 g (5½ oz)	None	No	2:00
Potatoes (whole)	200 g (7 oz, 1 medium)	Washed, rubbed with a little oil and pricked all over with a fork	No	7:00–8:00
Potatoes (diced or baby)	200 g (7 oz)	Washed	Yes	8:00
Runner beans	180 g (6½ oz)	De-stringed and chopped	Yes	5:00
Spinach (fresh, large leaf)	200 g (7 oz)	Washed	No	2:00
Squash	400 g (14 oz, 1 medium)	Peeled, de-seeded and diced	No	8:00
Sugar snap peas	150 g (5½ oz)	Washed and trimmed	No	2:00
Sweet potatoes	600 g (1 lb 5 oz, 2 medium)	Washed and pricked all over with a fork	No	10:00–12:00
Sweetcorn (on the cob)	4 ears	Shucked and trimmed	Yes	10:00

SIDE
THI

STARTERS AND SMALL SANDINGS

CHICKEN CRACKLING

**SERVES 2–3 AS A LITTLE BAR SNACK;
ALSO YIELDS ABOUT 50 G (1¾ OZ) CHICKEN FAT**

While chicken meat cooks quite nicely in the microwave, the same cannot be said for skin. Whack a skin-on thigh in the microwave and the skin will just sort of wither and die, becoming somehow both soft and rubbery. However! If you isolate the skin and cook it separately, it works amazingly well. The skin can be enjoyed on its own as a tasty snack, or scattered over other dishes for a bit of texture. It also yields a very useful by-product: chicken fat! This can be used in place of oil in recipes for added flavour, or used to enrich sauces and soups (such as the chicken ramen on page 102). These are best enjoyed within a few hours of cooking; the fat can be tipped into a jar and kept in the refrigerator for about a week.

---

roughly 150 g (5½ oz) raw chicken skin (this is about the weight of the skin from a whole medium chicken, except the wings, which are too fiddly to skin)

salt, MSG and/or any other dry seasonings you like

Place the skin in a bowl and cover very loosely. Cook for 12 minutes on power level 6, stirring a couple of times throughout cooking. The skin at this point should be golden brown, and swimming in a pool of golden fat. If not, keep cooking in 1-minute intervals until totally crisp. Remove the skin from the fat and drain on paper towel. Season as you like while still hot.

WARNING

Do not use a plastic container!
The hot fat can melt or damage
the plastic.

SQUASH WITH FETA, CRUSHED RASPBERRIES AND SAGE

SERVES 1 AS A SUBSTANTIAL LUNCH, OR 2 AS A SUBSTANTIAL SIDE

Remember the 90s? Everybody was dancing to awful ska-punk, and all of our food was covered in either pesto sauce or raspberry vinaigrette. At least, those were the 90s in America. I imagine here in the UK people were still probably eating mostly ship's biscuit and powdered eggs, with Italian restaurants just beginning to appear on high streets to offer tastes of exotic dishes like spaghetti and garlic bread. Anyway, I don't miss the 90s, nor do I miss raspberry vinaigrette, but I do like the idea of raspberries in savoury dishes, mainly as a substitute for the highly overrated pomegranate. Here it adds a similar sour-sweet flavour to the classic combination of squash, sage and feta. It's the rare kind of salad that not only tastes good hot or cold, but also holds up after a day or two in the refrigerator.

350 g (12 oz) squash (peeled weight), cut into roughly 2.5 cm (1 in) cubes	Toss everything together in a small-ish baking dish, cover and cook for 10 minutes, stirring halfway through cooking.
salt and black pepper	
a glug of olive oil	
1 teaspoon dried sage	

50 g (1¾ oz) raspberries (fresh or frozen, either is fine)	Combine everything in a small bowl and lightly crush the berries with a fork.
1 tablespoon caster (superfine) sugar	
1 tablespoon wine vinegar (red or white)	
1 tablespoon olive oil	

C

60–70 g (2–2½ oz) feta, coarsely crumbled	Leave the squash (A) to cool slightly, then toss with the feta and raspberry dressing (B). Scatter over the seeds or nuts to garnish.
a handful of pumpkin seeds, shelled pistachios or pine nuts	

GREEN BEANS WITH CHILLI, GARLIC, THAI BASIL AND BACON

SERVES 2—4

One of my all-time favourite Sichuanese dishes is dry-fried green beans, in which the humble legume is blasted with a salvo of flavour from minced (ground) pork, dried chillies, a bunch of other seasonings and a lick of smoke from the wok. This dish is not that (just go to your local Sichuanese restaurant for it, they'll do it better than you can anyway), but it has a similar flavour profile: spicy, fresh, oily, sweet and salty, delicious with rice as a light lunch, or as part of a larger meal.

A

2 slices of smoked streaky bacon

Follow the instructions for cooking two slices of bacon on page 34. Once the bacon is cooked, remove it from the plate and drain on paper towels. Don't throw away the rendered bacon fat. When the bacon is cool enough to handle, chop or break it into little bits.

B

150–200 g (5½–7 oz) green beans, trimmed

1 garlic clove, thinly sliced

1 small, fresh red chilli (any spice level or variety you like), thinly sliced

½ tablespoon honey

1 tablespoon soy sauce

1 teaspoon water

Tip a spoonful of the bacon fat into a bowl or container and add the beans, garlic, chilli, honey, soy sauce and water, and mix well. Cover and cook for 4 minutes, until the beans are tender but still have some bite to them.

C

a couple big pinches of sesame seeds, crushed

a handful of Thai basil, roughly torn

Stir the chopped bacon (A), crushed sesame and torn basil into the beans (B). Leave to rest for 1–2 minutes before serving so the basil wilts.

ASPARAGUS WITH TARRAGON VINAIGRETTE

SERVES 4

Asparagus is one of my favourite things to cook in the microwave, which is super simple and a great way to maintain their colour and crunch. They're great with just a bit of salt, of course, but with a good vinaigrette and some bread (and perhaps a poached egg) they make a pretty great meal all on their own.

2 tablespoons vegetable oil

1 tablespoon red wine vinegar (or whatever vinegar you like, really)

2 teaspoons honey

2 teaspoons wholegrain mustard

1 teaspoon lemon juice (from about ¼ lemon, if using fresh)

¼ teaspoon celery salt

½ banana shallot or 1 regular shallot, very finely chopped

several sprigs of tarragon, leaves picked and finely chopped

Combine everything in a jar and shake hard to bring the dressing together.

This is actually better made a day or two in advance, to allow the flavours to infuse – but remember to shake it again before serving.

500 g (1 lb 2 oz) asparagus, bases peeled or trimmed of woody bits

Place the asparagus in a bowl or baking dish, cover and cook for 3–5 minutes (depending on how done you like them), tossing halfway through cooking.

To serve, simply toss the asparagus through the vinaigrette (A). This can be enjoyed hot or cold.

ADDICTIVE BROCCOLI

SERVES 2—4

In Japan the word *yamitsuki* (addictive) is applied frequently to vegetable dishes with a surprising can't-stop-eating-them quality. I didn't set out to make this dish yamitsuki, but after I cooked it I couldn't stop returning to the bowl to snack on it while I prepared other things. The next thing I knew, I'd gotten one of my five-a-day!

Ⓐ

1 tablespoon olive oil

4 anchovy fillets

Combine the olive oil and anchovies in a large bowl or baking dish and cook, uncovered, for 30 seconds.

Ⓑ

1 head of broccoli, cut into florets (about 350 g/12 oz)

black pepper, to taste

1 tablespoon water

Break up the anchovies with a fork, then toss the broccoli through the oil along with the pepper and water. Cover, and cook for 4–5 minutes until cooked through but still with a good bite.

Ⓒ

juice of ½ lemon

a handful (about 15 g/½ oz) of toasted flaked (slivered) almonds

Squeeze over the lemon juice, toss and garnish with the almonds.

LOADED TWICE-BAKED POTATOES

SERVES 2—4

I associate this dish with American sports bars and family restaurant chains like TGI Friday's. But with the help of my microwave, I can now enjoy this delicious and versatile side without having to go to such awful, awful places.

A

4 slices of streaky bacon	Cook according to the instructions for four slices on page 34. Leave to cool, then coarsely chop.

B

2 baking potatoes, of average size	Rub the potatoes all over with olive oil and salt, and prick them several times with a fork. Place them on the same plate you used to cook the bacon, then cook for 10–12 minutes, turning them halfway through, until soft throughout. Leave to cool completely.
olive oil, as needed	
salt, as needed	

C

2 shakes of garlic granules	Cut the cooled potatoes (B) in half and scoop them out into a bowl, so you have four little potato skin 'boats' and a bowlful of soft, cooked potato. Mash the potato with all the remaining ingredients, but save a few pinches of chives to garnish. Taste and adjust seasoning as you like with salt.
black pepper, to taste	
¼ teaspoon dried dill	
50 g (1¾ oz) Red Leicester, grated	
50 g (1¾ oz/scant ¼ cups) sour cream	
1 teaspoon wholegrain or Dijon mustard	Spoon the mashed potato mixture back into the skins, then put them on a plate and cook, uncovered, for 7 minutes. To serve, garnish with the chopped bacon (A), chives and a pinch or two of paprika.
1 dash each of Worcestershire sauce and Tabasco sauce (both optional)	
salt, to taste	
a handful of chives, finely chopped	
a few pinches of paprika, plus extra for garnish	

FREEZER DUMPLINGS WITH CHILLI OIL AND SESAME SAUCE

SERVES 2—4

This started out as a recipe for making dumplings from scratch, but then I thought: this book is meant to save time and effort, and making dumplings is antithetical to this. By all means, make your own dumplings if you like, but pre-made frozen dumplings are delicious and extremely handy. (Oddly, if you do make your own dumplings, they actually cook better in the microwave if you freeze them first.) This recipe also contains a method for making your own chilli oil in the microwave. Why bother making your own chilli oil but not your own dumplings? Well, for one thing, it's very economical – homemade chilli oil is incredibly cheap compared to shop-bought versions. And it's also customisable – you can make it as spicy (or as not spicy) as you like by adjusting the amount of chilli you add.

4 tablespoons vegetable oil	Place the oil, garlic, shallot and ginger into a glass jug or dish, stir, and cook for 2–3 minutes until the aromatics sizzle and begin to brown. Add the chilli flakes and sesame seeds and stir well, then cook for another 30 seconds–1 minute. Leave to cool to room temperature, then stir in the sesame oil.

4 tablespoons vegetable oil

3 garlic cloves, finely chopped

1 small shallot, finely chopped

1 cm (½ in) fresh ginger root, thinly sliced

1 tablespoon hot chilli (hot pepper) flakes

1 teaspoon sesame seeds

1 tablespoon sesame oil

Place the oil, garlic, shallot and ginger into a glass jug or dish, stir, and cook for 2–3 minutes until the aromatics sizzle and begin to brown. Add the chilli flakes and sesame seeds and stir well, then cook for another 30 seconds–1 minute. Leave to cool to room temperature, then stir in the sesame oil.

4 tablespoons tahini or Chinese sesame paste

4 tablespoons soy sauce

2 tablespoons rice vinegar (ideally Chinkiang)

1 tablespoon sugar

½ garlic clove, finely grated

juice from ¼ lime (about 1 teaspoon)

Stir together all the ingredients until smooth and well mixed.

20 frozen dumplings (wontons, gyoza or similar)

1 tablespoon sesame oil

a few spring onions (scallions) and/or coriander (cilantro) leaves, finely sliced (optional)

Place the dumplings in a large bowl and add enough water to cover. Add the sesame oil and stir. Cover and cook for 8–10 minutes until the water has boiled and the dumplings are cooked through.

Place the sesame sauce (B) and chilli oil (A) into the bottom of a serving bowl or bowls, then use a slotted spoon to transfer the dumplings into the bowls. Mix well before eating. If you like, garnish with the spring onions and/or coriander.

WARNING

Do not use a plastic container to make the chilli oil! It can reach temperatures above boiling and melt or damage the plastic.

SCOTCH BONNET SUCCOTASH

SERVES UP TO 4

Succotash, a Southern vegetable dish traditionally based on lima beans and corn, is a great thing to have in your culinary repertoire because of its ease and versatility: it goes well with almost anything, and can take almost any vegetable. In this version I add a little bit of chopped Scotch bonnet, which jolts the whole thing into a higher gear of flavour with sparks of fruity heat and cherry-red colour. The use of thyme and allspice is inspired by seasonings used for Jamaican jerk. They are optional, but I think they turn this humble dish into something greater than the sum of its parts.

---

1 (bell) pepper, de-seeded and diced

1 tin (165 g/5¾ oz drained weight) of sweetcorn

4 spring onions (scallions), roughly chopped

120 g (4½ oz) frozen broad (fava) beans

1 small-ish Scotch bonnet or similar hot chilli, de-seeded and finely chopped

20 g (¾ oz) butter

⅛ teaspoon salt

¼ teaspoon allspice (optional)

4 sprigs of fresh thyme, or about ½ teaspoon dried thyme (optional)

Stir everything together in a medium bowl. Cook, uncovered, for 10 minutes, stirring halfway through cooking. Cook for 2–5 minutes, or longer if you prefer the vegetables softer; I like them pretty crunchy.

CHANGE IT UP!

Traditional additions to succotash include bacon, salt beef, tomatoes and/or okra. You can also substitute or supplement the broad (fava) beans with kidney beans, edamame or peas. I also like this with chopped runner beans or green beans.

NOTE This recipe uses frozen broad (fava) beans, straight from the freezer. If they are fresh or defrosted, reduce the cooking time.

BROWN BUTTER CORNBREAD WITH CHIPOTLE MASCARPONE

SERVES AT LEAST 8

It doesn't get much better than cornbread. It's basically polenta cake, all sunshine yellow and cereal-sweet but you eat it with savoury food. This one is based on brown butter for a nutty flavour, topped with mascarpone spiked with chipotle paste – the spicy-savoury icing on the corn cake.

150 g (5½ oz) butter	Place the butter into a 23 cm (9 in) square baking dish (ideally silicone, but glass is fine too – do not use plastic!) and loosely cover. Cook for 5–6 minutes until the butter melts completely and the milk solids brown. Tip the melted butter into a bowl and leave to cool slightly, then whisk in the honey, buttermilk and eggs.
80 g (2¾ oz/scant ¼ cup) honey	
150 ml (5 fl oz/scant ⅔ cup) buttermilk or plain yoghurt	
4 eggs	

250 g (9 oz/generous 1½ cups) fine polenta (cornmeal)	Add all the ingredients to the butter mixture (A) and mix well. Tip the batter back into the baking dish, cover and cook for 10 minutes.
120 g (4¼ oz/scant 1 cup) plain (all-purpose) flour	
1½ teaspoons baking powder	
½ teaspoon bicarbonate of soda (baking soda)	
½ teaspoon salt	
2 spring onions (scallions), chopped	
1 small tin (180–200 g/6½–7 oz) of sweetcorn, drained	

50 g (1¾ oz) chipotle paste	Beat together the chipotle paste and mascarpone until smooth. When the cornbread (B) is done, leave to cool slightly before serving. Slice and serve with dollops of the chipotle mascarpone on top.
150 g (5½ oz) mascarpone	

WARNING
Do not use a plastic container to make the brown butter! It can reach temperatures above boiling and melt or damage the plastic.

CHEAT'S COWBOY BEANS

SERVES 4–8

After 15 years in the UK, I still haven't completely acquired the taste for British baked beans. I can't help but compare them to the American baked beans I grew up with, and the comparison is not favourable. Ours are fortified with a variety of inherently delicious seasonings, like black treacle (molasses), bacon and warming spices. Baked beans that take these seasonings in the direction of a chilli con carne – and indeed, may actually add carne in the form of minced (ground) beef – are called cowboy beans, though I don't think actual cowboys ever ate them. These can be time-consuming to make, but the good news is, even though British baked beans are pretty meh, they can be gussied up easily to make something similar to cowboy beans. I'm not sure if I would bring them to a barbecue in Texas, but they do satisfy my American bean craving whenever it strikes. They're usually a side dish, of course, but because they're so substantial they can also be a meal on their own.

A

15 g (½ oz) butter, dripping or lard

1 onion, diced

1 (bell) pepper, diced

Combine the fat, onion and pepper in a large bowl. Cover and cook for 7 minutes, stirring halfway through cooking.

B

250 g (9 oz) smoked gammon or very thick-cut smoked bacon, diced

Stir in the gammon or bacon, re-cover and cook for 4 minutes.

C

2 x 400 g (14 oz) tins of British baked beans

1 tablespoon smoked paprika

1 tablespoon dark brown sugar

1 tablespoon ketchup

1 tablespoon soy sauce

1 tablespoon Worcestershire sauce

½ teaspoon vinegar (any kind)

lots of black pepper

hot chilli sauce, to taste

Stir in all of the remaining ingredients except the chilli sauce and cook, uncovered, for 12 minutes, stirring halfway through. Taste and adjust the flavour as you like with hot sauce (I think a good dose of chilli really makes this).

BRAISED RED CABBAGE

SERVES 2—4

The Bizarro World counterpart to the nonsense that is 'pan-Asian' food, would, of course, be 'pan-European' food. No such thing really exists, of course, but if it did it would probably be a lot easier to pin down than 'pan-Asian'. One could take a reductionist view, as in the case of Yanko Tsvetkov's satirical *Atlas of Prejudice*, which simply divides the continent into 'Potato Europe' and 'Tomato Europe'. But I think it's more fun to try and find true universals. I posed this question on Facebook some time ago: what would be the key flavours of pan-European cookery? The responses included cheese, bread, beer, sausage, apples and one I don't fully agree with but still find intriguing: dill.

I would also add to that list braised red cabbage. I think almost every European country has some variation of it, and it goes with every European dish. Sausage and mash? Braised red cabbage. Cassoulet? Braised red cabbage. Pierogies? Braised red cabbage. Goulash? Braised red cabbage. Carbonara? Maybe not carbonara. But Italy does actually have its own braised red cabbage dishes, like *cavolo rosso in agrodolce*, from the south, and *cavolo rosso stufato*, from the north. I actually didn't know that! See? Across Europe, braised red cabbage comes from anywhere and everywhere – and now, it can even come from your microwave.

---

400 g (14 oz) red cabbage (about ½ cabbage), cored and thinly sliced

1 banana shallot or 2 regular shallots, peeled and thinly sliced

1 teaspoon cornflour (cornstarch)

a handful of fresh thyme or 1 bay leaf

1 tablespoon caraway seeds

4 tablespoons sherry or port

4 tablespoons red wine

4 tablespoons water

1 tablespoon brown sugar (any kind)

1 tablespoon soy sauce

1 teaspoon wine vinegar (any kind)

1 teaspoon Marmite or Bovril

1 stock cube, crumbled (any kind)

Toss the cabbage and the shallot with the cornflour in a large bowl. Add all of the remaining ingredients and mix well. Cover loosely and cook for 20 minutes, stirring twice throughout cooking, then uncover and cook for another 10 minutes, stirring again halfway through. Discard the thyme or bay leaf before eating. This can be enjoyed hot or cold, and is even tastier after a night in the refrigerator.

BUTTERY BUTTER BEANS

SERVES 2

Butter beans have butter in their name for a reason. This recipe simply builds
upon their velvety richness with ordinary ingredients you probably already have.
This is a dish you can sink into like a goose down pillow (but a lot cheaper).
And because it's so pleasingly bland, it goes with everything – roast lamb,
steamed fish, sausage, greens – it's all good.

1 × 400 g (14 oz) tin of butter beans,
plus the liquid from the tin

about 7.5 cm (3 in) leek (the part towards
the base), finely sliced

3 garlic cloves, finely chopped

25 g (1 oz) butter

2 tablespoons double (heavy) cream

2 tablespoons white wine

1 teaspoon light brown sugar

¼ teaspoon salt

3 mint leaves, very finely sliced

a dollop of plain yoghurt

Combine everything, except the mint and
yoghurt, in a medium bowl, stir well, cover
and cook for 10 minutes, stirring halfway
through cooking. Uncover, stir again and cook
for 5 more minutes. Leave to cool for a minute
or two, then stir in the mint and yoghurt.

WHITE NECTARINE, HONEY AND ROSEWATER JAM

MAKES ABOUT 500 G/400 ML
(1 LB 2 OZ/13 FL OZ/GENEROUS 1½ CUPS)

Nectarines and peaches make such a lovely jam; I don't know why it isn't more common. It's even good made with fruits that are only so-so on their own – and in fact, it's better to use slightly under-ripe nectarines for this because they contain more pectin. This is delicious however you'd use jam in general, but I think it is particularly good with creamy, mild cheese.

1 teaspoon olive oil

500 g (1 lb 2 oz, stoned weight; about 4–5 fruits) white nectarines, stones removed

3 tablespoons lemon juice (from about 1½ lemons)

200 g (7 oz/scant 1 cup) caster (superfine) sugar

100 g (3½ oz/scant ⅓ cup) honey

1–2 teaspoons rosewater (to taste)

Tip the olive oil into a large glass bowl and rub it all over the surface of the bowl – this will help prevent overboiling. Coarsely chop the nectarines. (Leave their skins on – they'll soften completely during cooking and provide a gorgeous colour to the jam.) Place them in the bowl along with the lemon juice, sugar and honey, and stir well. Cover with a microwave-safe plate and cook for 25–30 minutes, stirring halfway through cooking, until the jam sets when spooned onto a chilled plate. (If you have a thermometer, it should reach 105°C/221°F.) Once the jam is finished cooking, leave to cool for a few minutes, then stir in the rosewater. Transfer to a sterilised jar and keep in the refrigerator. It will keep for at least a year.

WARNING

Do not use a plastic container to make this! It can melt or damage the plastic.

ROASTED SHALLOTS AND FENNEL

SERVES UP TO 4

I had some fennel. I had some shallots. I had a microwave. Sometimes dishes don't have interesting backstories or clever flavour combinations. Sometimes they're just good and simple. Serve this however you wish; it would be excellent with all sorts of roast dinners, in warm salads with squash and ancient grains, or stirred through pasta. When I tested it I had it with smoked haddock (also steamed in the microwave, page 90) and risotto (page 86) and it was a perfect meal.

1 medium fennel bulb (200–250 g/7–9 oz), halved and cut into 1 cm (½ in) thick slices

6 banana shallots, peeled, trimmed and halved lengthways

6 tablespoons olive oil

fine salt, as needed (to taste)

a sprig or two of fresh thyme or rosemary, or a few pinches of dried thyme or rosemary

juice of 1 lemon or a glug of vinegar (any kind)

sea salt, to taste (optional)

Combine all of the ingredients, except the lemon or vinegar and sea salt (if using), in a large bowl and toss well. Cover and cook on power level 6 for 10 minutes, then stir, re-cover and cook for another 8 minutes on full power. Leave to cool slightly before serving. To serve, toss with lemon juice or whatever vinegar you like, and sprinkle with a little sea salt, if you've got it.

CREAMED SPINACH

Whenever my wife and I get a night out to ourselves, we almost always go out for steak. London has one of the most diverse restaurant cultures in the world, but the low-key luxury of a good, old school steakhouse is hard for us to resist when we're treating ourselves. And it's not just about the steak – it's about the cocktails and red wine, the cushy banquettes and, crucially, the sides. And the king of the steakhouse sides is creamed spinach – just about as indulgent as the steak itself. Pro tip: a good creamed spinach is also the best sauce for steak. Sorry not sorry peppercorn and béarnaise.

 A

15 g (½ oz) butter	Whisk everything together in a bowl or gratin dish until no lumps of flour remain (don't worry about the butter). Cook, uncovered, for 1 minute, then whisk again and cook for another minute, to form a smooth, thick white sauce.
2 tablespoons plain (all-purpose) flour	
1 teaspoon cornflour (cornstarch)	
lots of grated or ground nutmeg	
several grinds of white pepper	
90 ml (3 fl oz/6 tablespoons) whole milk	

 B

250 g (9 oz) frozen spinach	Stir in the frozen spinach and garlic, cover and cook for 7 minutes, stirring halfway through. Stir in the double cream and salt, then taste and adjust seasoning as you like.
2 garlic cloves, grated or thinly sliced	
2 tablespoons double (heavy) cream	
salt, to taste	

 C

20 g (¾ oz) Swiss cheese (such as Gruyère or Emmental), grated	Top the spinach with the cheeses and cook, uncovered, for 2 minutes until fully melted. Serve piping hot.
10 g (½ oz) Parmesan, grated	

SWEET POTATOES AND PARSNIPS WITH RAS EL HANOUT, SATSUMA AND CHILLI

SERVES 2—4

A couple of Christmases ago, my brother gave me a packet of ras el hanout, the complex North African seasoning typically featuring a mixture of warm, sweet spices such as cinnamon, clove and pepper along with more floral, fragrant ones such as rose, galangal and cardamom. As someone who mainly cooks Japanese and American food I was initially clueless about what to do with ras el hanout, but I soon found myself reaching for it as a versatile flavour enhancer wherever a touch of spice is welcome. Here, the spice is accented by a little bit of orange and chilli – and actually, you don't need ras el hanout to make it. Mixed spice, five-spice powder or even just cinnamon will provide a similar effect.

A

25 g (1 oz) butter

1 teaspoon ras el hanout or similar warm, sweet spices

¼–½ teaspoon chilli (hot pepper) flakes

2 tablespoons sunflower seeds

Place the butter in a baking dish, cover loosely and cook for 1 minute to melt. Add the spices and the sunflower seeds, stir and cook, uncovered, for 1–2 minutes.

B

1 large (about 300 g/10½ oz) sweet potato, scrubbed clean and cut into large wedges

about 300 g (10½ oz) parsnips, peeled and cut into chunks about the same size as the potato wedges

1 satsuma, halved

salt, to taste

Add the vegetables to the dish and squeeze in the juice of the satsuma, then chuck in the squeezed-out peels as well. Season well with salt and toss. Cook, covered, for 10 minutes, followed by 10 minutes uncovered, tossing a few times throughout the cooking. Discard the satsumas before serving.

MAC AND CHEESE

SERVES UP TO 4

Mac and cheese, along with ramen and perhaps crab cocktail, is a perennial contender for my last meal. (I'd probably have all three.) It was the first dish I ever cooked – from a box, but there was a pan to wash up after, so it still counts. It's a dish I have cooked many, many ways over many, many years, but truthfully, have never quite perfected. Maybe I will someday. For now, here's a recipe that comes close – tender macaroni in a silky smooth, very slightly stringy sauce, with a pure but not overwhelming cheese flavour.

200 g (7 oz) macaroni

500 ml (16 fl oz/2 cups) water

100 g (4½ oz) evaporated milk

40 g (1½ oz) butter

Stir everything together in a large bowl and cook, covered, for 16 minutes, stirring halfway through cooking.

4 slices of American (processed) cheese, roughly torn

40 g (1½ oz) medium or mild (not mature) Red Leicester, grated

40 g (1½ oz) mozzarella, grated

40 g (1½ oz) mild Swiss cheese (such as Emmental), grated

10 g (½ oz) Parmesan or similar, grated

salt and black pepper, to taste

Stir in the American cheese, re-cover and cook for another 2 minutes. Stir in all the remaining cheeses until melted, then cook for 1 more minute. Stir again, taste and adjust the seasoning as you like with salt and pepper.

TIP This recipe works with pre-grated shop-bought cheese, but it is a little better with freshly grated cheese as this does not have any added starch.

CHANGE IT UP!

For me, the simplicity of a pure, no frills mac and cheese is hard to beat. But I am not opposed to additions. Some of my favourites are:

JALAPEÑOS

Use fresh or pickled, very finely chopped – add about halfway through cooking.

MUSHROOMS AND SAUSAGE

The mushrooms should be sliced, and the sausage crumbled, both added about halfway through cooking; the mushrooms will release additional water, so reduce the amount in the recipe to 450 ml (15 fl oz/ scant 2 cups).

BROCCOLI

Cut into bite-size pieces and add about halfway through cooking. This is especially nice with rarebit seasonings like mustard and Worcestershire sauce.

HAM OR CHICKEN AND PEAS

Toss ham or cooked chicken and frozen peas in towards the end of cooking to make this into something vaguely resembling a balanced main meal.

WE HOLD THESE MAC & CHEESE TRUTHS TO BE SELF-EVIDENT

1.

The best mac and cheese is based on the pasta cooking water, never on a roux, which is too thick and too bland.

2.

If you are put off by evaporated milk and American cheese, you can never know true mac and cheese happiness.

3.

Slightly overcooked pasta is not only acceptable but perhaps even preferable.

4.

The best mac and cheese is only slightly more flavourful than something you can make from a box – we do not want super-sharp, funky cheese flavours, just smooth, creamy comfort.

PRAWNS WITH GARLIC BUTTER AND BREADCRUMBS

SERVES 2

When I was growing up, prawns (shrimp) with garlic butter represented the peak of luxury. We only had it at restaurants that were too expensive to be part of our regular rotation, like Red Lobster, or on my dad's birthday. Nowadays, this still feels like a real treat – give me a plate of these and I'll be happy as a clam. (This recipe also works, by the way, with clams.) This is inspired in particular by an old-school Chicago dish called shrimp de Jonghe, which uses a technique not often seen any more: using soft breadcrumbs to thicken the sauce and help it cling to the prawns.

A

20 g (¾ oz/¼ cups) breadcrumbs

Tip the breadcrumbs into a medium baking dish (about 20–23 cm (8–9 in) in diameter) and cook in 1-minute intervals, stirring after each interval until they are evenly and lightly toasted – this should take about 4 minutes total. Tip out the crumbs and set them aside.

B

30 g (1 oz) butter

4 garlic cloves, grated

200 g (7 oz) raw shelled prawns (shrimp)

salt and black pepper, to taste

zest from about ½ lemon (optional)

Add the butter and garlic to the dish and cover loosely, then cook for 1 minute so the butter fully melts. Stir in about half of the breadcrumbs (set aside from part A) along with the prawns, a pinch of salt and pepper, and the lemon zest (if using). Cover and cook for 1 minute 30 seconds–2 minutes, until the prawns are steamed through.

C

a few basil leaves, finely chopped (optional)

Stir in the basil (if using) and garnish with the remaining breadcrumbs (set aside from part A) and a little more pepper.

CRAB AND ARTICHOKE GRATIN

SERVES 2 AT A VERY MINIMUM,
AND UP TO 8 AS A SHARER

This decadent dish can be enjoyed as a party snack or as something shared between two or three people as a dinner. In true 60s throwback recipe fashion, it's outstanding with an ice-cold martini.

200–250 g (7–9 oz) tinned artichoke hearts (drained weight)

100 g (3½ oz) crab meat – any kind (fake, tinned, fresh), but I like a 50/50 mix of white and dark meat

½ teaspoon Old Bay, Cajun seasoning or similar all-purpose seasoning

a few dashes of Tabasco sauce or similar

1 garlic clove, grated

4 tablespoons double (heavy) cream

a handful of tarragon leaves, flat-leaf parsley leaves or chives, finely chopped

Ensure the artichokes are very well drained – you may want to gently press them in a sieve (fine mesh strainer) or colander to ensure they don't have much excess water in them.

Very roughly chop the artichokes, then stir them together in a gratin dish with everything else, reserving a pinch of the chopped herbs to use later as a garnish. Cook, uncovered, for 4 minutes.

60 g (2 oz) Swiss cheese, grated

40 g (1½ oz) medium Cheddar, grated

black pepper, to taste

Scatter the cheeses and a few grinds of pepper over the crab and artichoke mixture. Cook for 2–3 more minutes, uncovered, until the cheeses are fully melted, then garnish with the chopped herbs set aside in part A.

crusty bread or chunky crackers, to serve

Serve the gratin (B) piping hot, with crackers or bread on the side for dipping.

TIP   Don't use artichokes in oil from a jar for this – the soft tinned ones are preferable because they break down well during cooking

STEAMED AUBERGINE SALAD WITH SMOKY LIME AND FISH SAUCE DRESSING

SERVES 2

One of my favourite Thai dishes is *yum makhua yao*, or smoky aubergine (eggplant) salad. Traditionally, the aubergine gets its smokiness from charring over flames, which of course we cannot do in the microwave. (If your microwave is capable of flame-grilling, please return it to the manufacturer.) However, we can achieve the same soft and squishy texture by microwave steaming, and add the smoky flavour in the form of paprika – not traditional, of course, but neither is cooking this in the microwave. This recipe is informed primarily by John Chantarasak's version from his excellent book *Kin Thai* – please do check it out if you haven't already!

2 tablespoons light brown sugar

juice of 1 lime (about 1 tablespoon)

1 tablespoon fish sauce

½ teaspoon smoked paprika

1 bird's eye or similar small, hot chilli, very thinly sliced

1 garlic clove, very thinly sliced

Stir everything together until the sugar dissolves. This is best made at least an hour in advance to allow the flavours to mingle.

B

1 aubergine (eggplant)

Cut the aubergine into quarters lengthways, so you have four long baton-shaped pieces. Bundle these pieces up and wrap them in cling film (plastic wrap), then cook for 4–6 minutes, turning the bundle once during cooking. The aubergines should be totally soft, so if there are any firm bits, keep cooking for 1–2 minutes. Transfer to the refrigerator to chill (this will take at least an hour).

1 shallot or ½ banana shallot, very thinly sliced with the grain

2 small tomatoes, quartered

generous handfuls of mint and coriander (cilantro) leaves

1 fresh lime leaf, very, very, very thinly sliced (optional)

a few crispy shallots (optional; see method, page 33)

To serve, unwrap the chilled aubergines (B) and lay on a plate. Scatter over the raw shallots, tomatoes and fresh herbs, then pour over the dressing (A) and top with a few crispy shallots (if using).

STEAMED MANGETOUT AND PEPPERS WITH TAHINI DRESSING

SERVES 2

Mangetout (snow peas) are one of my favourite things to microwave, as at home in a salad as they are on top of a bowl of noodles or alongside meat or fish. With some just-cooked crunchy peppers, they make a simple, satisfying, vibrant side which can be enjoyed hot or cold.

Ⓐ

2 tablespoons tahini

2 tablespoons plain yoghurt

1 tablespoon lemon juice

1 teaspoon honey

½ garlic clove, grated

a generous pinch of salt

Combine everything and mix well to make a smooth dressing.

Ⓑ

150 g (5½ oz) mangetout (snow peas)

1 red (bell) pepper, de-seeded and sliced

1 teaspoon olive oil

a pinch of salt

Toss the mangetout and pepper with the olive oil and a pinch of salt in a wide bowl or baking dish, then cook, uncovered, for 4 minutes. Leave the vegetables to cool slightly before dressing (they can also be served cold).

Ⓒ

a few pinches of black and/or white sesame seeds, to garnish

a pinch of mild chilli (hot pepper) flakes or powder, to garnish (optional)

Drizzle the dressing (A) over the cooked vegetables (B) and garnish with a sprinkling of sesame seeds and chilli flakes, if you like.

MARMITE AND BOURSIN DEVILLED MUSHROOMS

SERVES 2

Devilling is a dying art. I'd like to see more devilling. When's the last time you devilled something? I'll bet it was an egg, or *maybe* kidneys, and I'll bet it was a while ago. To get you back on your devilling game, here's a super simple, super delicious mushroom recipe, with a tangy, slightly spicy sauce based on Boursin, Marmite and the mushrooms' own umami-tastic juices. These are great on crusty bread but also on pasta or as a side dish for roast chicken or beef.

20 g (¾ oz) butter

1 teaspoon Marmite

½ teaspoon mustard (English or wholegrain)

2 garlic cloves, grated

1–2 dashes of hot sauce

1–2 dashes of Worcestershire sauce

300 g (10½ oz) button or chestnut mushrooms, cleaned

a few sprigs of flat-leaf parsley, chopped

30 g (1 oz) Boursin or similar

Place the butter in a medium bowl and cook for 15–30 seconds to melt. Stir in the Marmite, mustard, garlic, hot sauce and Worcestershire sauce, then tip in the mushrooms and toss them well. Cook, uncovered, for 5 minutes, stirring twice throughout the cooking. When finished, stir in the parsley and Boursin, melting the cheese to form a thick, creamy sauce.

BURRATA WITH LIGHTLY CONFITED TOMATOES, PINE NUTS AND SHICHIMI

SERVES 4

Burrata is a blank slate for flavour – its sweet, creamy blandness is amenable to so many accompaniments. (Caponata, page 130, is an excellent one, for example.) Here it is paired with cherry tomatoes lightly cooked with garlic in oil, plus toasted pine nuts and shichimi tōgarashi (a Japanese chilli-based spice blend). But any kind of crunchy nut and chilli powder or flakes will work – and actually you don't need them at all! It's delicious enough with just the tomatoes. Similarly, if you can't get burrata, then a nice ball of mozzarella will do, or even silken tofu.

220 g (7¾ oz) cherry or baby plum tomatoes, halved	Stir everything together in a small bowl. Cook, uncovered, for 3 minutes, stirring halfway through cooking. Transfer to the refrigerator to chill completely.
2 tablespoons olive oil	
1 garlic clove, thinly sliced	
a pinch of dried oregano	
a good pinch of salt	

20 g (¾ oz/⅛ cup) pine nuts	Place the nuts on a flat plate and toss with a pinch of salt. Cook for 2 minutes, stirring the nuts halfway through cooking. Continue to cook in 30-second intervals until the nuts are aromatic and lightly coloured, stirring each time, then continuing in 15-second intervals until they are nicely browned all over. Set aside to cool.
a pinch of salt	

C

2 burrata or big mozzarella balls, drained	When the tomatoes (A) are cold and the nuts (B) are cool, spoon the tomatoes onto serving dishes and top with the burrata and the pine nuts. Sprinkle over the sea salt and shichimi. You can have this with bread, if you like, but I just like it by itself.
a couple generous pinches of sea salt flakes	
shichimi tōgarashi or similar chilli blend, to taste	
crusty bread, to serve (optional)	

MUSSEL AND BELGIAN ALE CHOWDER

SERVES 2

This is a hearty soup/stew based on the classic combination of mussels and Belgian ale. You can use just about any golden Belgian ale you like, really, though I've used a witbier, with notes of orange and coriander. While this is in the 'small dish' chapter, as that's where soups usually go, with a simple veg side and some bread this can be a meal on its own.

Ⓐ

100 ml (3½ fl oz/scant ½ cup) Belgian ale (golden ales, saisons or witbiers work best)

2 tablespoons double (heavy) cream

2 banana shallots, diced

2 garlic cloves, thinly sliced

1 bay leaf (optional)

4–5 black peppercorns (optional)

200 g (7 oz) new potatoes, washed and cut into roughly 1 cm (½ in) thick pieces

Combine all the ingredients in a large bowl or baking dish. Cover and cook for 10 minutes until the potatoes are soft.

Ⓑ

10 g (½ oz) butter

500 g (1 lb 2 oz) mussels, cleaned and trimmed of any beards, with broken or open shells discarded

Add the butter and mussels, re-cover and cook for 5 minutes until the mussels' shells have opened and the meat has steamed through. Discard any unopened mussels.

Ⓒ

a big pinch of dried dill (optional)

a handful of flat-leaf parsley or tarragon leaves, chopped

crusty bread, to serve (optional)

Stir the herbs through the hot soup. Serve on its own or with bread to make a substantial meal.

SWEETCORN WITH SOUR CREAM, CHEESE, CHILLI AND LIME

SERVES 2

This is inspired by Mexican *elotes*, barbecued corn which is then slathered in a mixture of sour cream and mayo, and seasoned with liberal amounts of chilli sauce, grated or crumbled cheese, and fresh lime. This recipe mainly differs from the real deal by being very much not barbecued – but it's still tasty nonetheless, and how could it not be? This power-team of toppings are so delicious they could make masking tape taste good, so imagine how they are on steamed sweetcorn, which is already considerably more delicious than masking tape.

A

2 teaspoons soy sauce

2 ears of corn, shucked and cleaned

Rub the soy sauce into each corn cob so it sinks into the kernels. Place the corn on a plate and cover, then cook for 5 minutes, turning the corn over halfway through cooking.

B

2 tablespoons sour cream

1 heaped tablespoon mayonnaise

¼ teaspoon smoked paprika

While the corn is cooking, stir together the sour cream, mayo and paprika until smooth.

C

about 30 g (1 oz) cotija, feta, pecorino, Wensleydale or similar dry, salty cheese, grated or finely crumbled

many dashes of hot sauce

½ lime

chilli (hot pepper) flakes or powder, to taste

When the corn (A) is done, uncover it and let it cool slightly, then slather it in the sour cream mayo mixture. Top with the cheese and hot sauce, then squeeze over the lime and sprinkle with as much chilli as you like.

MA

INS

PEA AND SMOKED MACKEREL RISOTTO WITH LEMON

SERVES 2 AS A MAIN, 4 AS A SIDE

I don't know how risotto got its reputation for being difficult to make. Is it because you're supposed to stand there like an automaton, stirring it until you die of old age or boredom? That's not difficult, it's just tedious. And you don't even have to do it! You can just whack it in the microwave. (Or the pressure cooker! I heard it cooks in 5 minutes. But this is not a pressure cooking book.)

A

40 g (1½ oz) butter

10 cm (4 in) leek, finely diced

2 garlic cloves, finely chopped

1 celery stalk, finely diced

Place the butter in a large bowl and cook for 30 seconds to melt, then add the leek, garlic and celery. Stir, cover and cook for 4 minutes, stirring again halfway through cooking.

B

150 g/180 ml (5½ oz/6 fl oz/¾ cup) short-grain (risotto) rice

540 ml (18 fl oz/2¼ cups) fish, chicken or veg stock

2 tablespoons white wine

Add the rice, stock and wine. Stir, re-cover and cook for 16 minutes, stirring once halfway through cooking.

C

zest of ½ lemon

100 g (3½ oz) peas

lots of black pepper

1 smoked mackerel fillet (about 150 g/5½ oz), skinless and boneless, broken into big chunks

60 g (2 oz) cream cheese

30 g (1 oz) Parmesan, grated

salt

a few sprigs of mint or dill, roughly chopped

Add the lemon zest, peas, black pepper and mackerel. Stir, re-cover and cook for another minute, then stir in the cheeses and cook for another minute. Taste and adjust the seasoning with salt and pepper. Spoon into shallow bowls and garnish with the mint or dill.

STEAMED SALMON AND PAK CHOI WITH SWEET SOY SAUCE AND FRESH GINGER

SERVES 4

My wife likes to joke about her limited cooking repertoire. In reality, she's a competent cook and can make many delicious things, but she'll tell you she can only make Japanese curry, cottage pie, pasta, flapjacks, and pan-fried salmon and pak choi (bok choi) with soy sauce, mirin and ginger. If she has a signature dish, it's probably that one. Salmon and pak choi steam beautifully in the microwave, and it can be used to cook starch-thickened sauces, like this, too. So here's my homage to Laura's signature salmon, in microwaved form.

1 tablespoon light brown sugar

5 tablespoons soy sauce

5 tablespoons apple juice

2 tablespoons mirin

2 teaspoons cornflour (cornstarch)

1 garlic clove, peeled and smashed

a few grinds of black pepper

Combine all the ingredients in a bowl and stir well, ensuring there are no un-dissolved clumps of cornflour. Cook, uncovered, for 3 minutes, stirring halfway through cooking, until the mixture boils and thickens. Leave to cool and infuse while you prepare the rest of the dish.

2 pak choi (bok choi), washed and quartered

Place the pak choi in a baking dish and cover loosely. Cook for 3–4 minutes, or until the leaves are slightly wilted and bright green in colour. Remove the pak choi from the dish and set aside, then tip out any water in the dish.

4 salmon fillets (500 g/1 lb 2 oz), skinned and de-boned

2.5 cm (1 in) fresh ginger root, peeled and very finely julienned

1–2 spring onions (scallions), finely sliced

a drizzle of sesame oil or chilli oil (optional)

2 lemon or lime wedges

Place the salmon in the dish, then pour the sauce on top of it. Cover and cook for 2 minutes. Turn the salmon over, then top with the ginger and pak choi. Re-cover and cook for another 2 minutes until the salmon is cooked through. Garnish with the spring onions, sesame or chilli oil, if you like, and fresh lemon or lime on the side to squeeze over at the table.

SMOKED HADDOCK EN PAPILLOTE WITH CAPERS AND OLIVES

SERVES 2

'En papillote' is one of those weird French cooking terms that has stuck with me, even though there's really no reason to keep using French for it – it just means 'in parchment'. (See also: *jus*. Why don't we just say 'juice'?) Anyway, it's simply a method of steaming food within a baking parchment or foil parcel, which is actually unnecessary in the microwave – ordinary containers do the same thing – but I gotta say, I love the theatre of food cooked this way. Opening up the parchment is like unwrapping a little present.

½ red (bell) pepper, very thinly sliced

1 garlic clove, very thinly sliced

8–10 pitted black olives, roughly chopped

a couple spoonfuls of capers

2 smoked haddock fillets (200–250 g/7–9 oz), boneless and either skinless or scaled

a couple drizzles of olive oil

a couple little splashes of white wine

a little bit of flat-leaf parsley or dill, chopped

Cut two large squares of parchment, as wide as the roll of baking parchment itself. Lay a little mound of the sliced peppers, garlic, olives and capers in the middle of each one, then place a haddock fillet on top of each mound. Add a drizzle of oil and a tiny splash of white wine to each fillet. Add the parsley or dill, then fold up the sides of the parchment over the fish like an envelope, then gather up the other sides and bundle them together as if you're packing a paper bag. Use a small wooden skewer or a toothpick to keep the bundle closed (poke it through the parchment just below the bundled-up top, which will be too thick to punch through).

Place the parcels on a plate and cook for 5 minutes. Serve in the parcels, to be unwrapped at the table.

SOUTHERN-STYLE SEAFOOD BOIL

SERVES AT LEAST 4, AND UP TO 6

This recipe is an homage to Tom Browne's Decatur, who began selling glorious Louisiana-style shrimp boils as meal kits during the first lockdown. Decatur's boils are a masterclass in, you know, boiling, and as it happens our old friend the microwave is excellent at boiling stuff. So, here is a Cajun-ish, Decatur-inspired seafood boil you can make in the microwave. Is it as good as Decatur's? Of course not, but that's not really the microwave's fault. It's just because Decatur is the best.
You will need a 3 litre (101 fl oz/12 cup) bowl for this recipe.

1 lemon, halved	Squeeze the lemon and orange into a large bowl, and chuck in the squeezed-out rinds along with the water, garlic, Cajun seasoning, stock cube and potatoes. Stir, cover and cook for 12 minutes until the potatoes are fork-tender.
½ orange or 1 satsuma, halved	
800 ml (27 fl oz/3⅓ cups) water	
1 garlic bulb, halved	
2 heaped tablespoons Cajun seasoning (plus more to serve)	
1 stock cube (any kind)	
300 g (12 oz) baby new potatoes	

2 smoky sausages, cut into 2.5 cm (1 in) chunks	Add the sausage and corn, stir, re-cover and cook for another 10 minutes. (Don't worry if some ingredients aren't submerged – they'll still cook through.) Add the shellfish and herbs, stir, cover and cook for another 10 minutes, tossing everything halfway through. If you are using clams or mussels, check to make sure they have all opened – any that haven't should be removed and thrown away. Leave the bowl covered while you prepare the garlic butter.
2 corn cobs, shucked and cleaned and cut into 5 cm (2 in) thick chunks	
1 kg (2 lb 4 oz) shellfish – you can go with all raw prawns (shrimp) (tail on are best), or use a mix of prawns, clams, mussels, squid or crab legs	
a handful of flat-leaf parsley, thyme and/or tarragon leaves	

50 g (1¾ oz) salted butter	Combine the butter and garlic in a jug, cover and cook for 1 minute 30 seconds, stirring halfway through.
2 garlic cloves, grated	To serve, tip all of the seafood, corn, sausages and potatoes into a wide tray along with about half of the cooking liquid. Season everything well with more Cajun seasoning. Serve with the garlic butter and hot sauce on the side, for people to add as they like.
Crystal hot sauce or similar (Tabasco or Frank's are fine), to serve	

TIP   Real-deal Louisianan seafood boils use Andouille sausage, which you are unlikely to find in the UK – a thick, smoky Polish sausage is the best substitute, but any flavourful sausage will do.

FISH PIE MIX COCONUT CURRY

SERVES 4

This is a mellow and aromatic curry made with fish pie mix,
one of the most economical sources of tasty fish there is. It's loosely based
on Maunika Gowardhan's Keralan fish moilee recipe from her excellent
book *Thali*, which you should absolutely check out.

A

2 tablespoons vegetable oil

about 2.5 cm (1 in) fresh ginger root, peeled and finely grated

½ onion, grated or finely chopped

4 cardamom pods, crushed

1 finger chilli, split down the middle

1 small tomato (about 80 g/2¾ oz), grated (and peel discarded)

½ lemongrass stalk, halved lengthways and bashed with a blunt object (optional)

a few fresh curry leaves or lime leaves, torn, or a handful of dried curry leaves (optional)

Combine the oil, ginger and onion in a large bowl and cook, covered, for 4 minutes, stirring halfway through. Add the cardamom, chilli, tomato, lemongrass and curry leaves or lime leaves (if using), stir, cover and cook for another 2 minutes.

B

1 teaspoon mild curry powder

1 × 400 g (14 oz) tin of coconut milk

1 tablespoon fish sauce

500 g (1 lb 2 oz) baby new potatoes, washed and halved

Add the curry powder, coconut milk, fish sauce and potatoes, re-cover and cook for 12 minutes until the potatoes are soft. Retrieve five or six of the potato pieces from the liquid and mash them in a separate bowl, then return the mash to the curry and stir well (this will help thicken and bind the sauce).

C

a big handful of coriander (cilantro) leaves, finely chopped

300–350 g (10½–12 oz) fish pie mix

salt, to taste

1 lime, quartered

Add most of the coriander and the fish pie mix, and stir well. Cover and cook for 2–3 minutes until the fish is just poached through. Taste and adjust the seasoning with salt as needed. Serve with the remaining coriander on top and lime wedges on the side. Good with rice or parathas!

CURRIED SMOKED HADDOCK OMELETTE

SERVES 2

This is inspired by two classic smoked haddock dishes, omelette Arnold Bennett and kedgeree. It is essentially a rich, cream-laden omelette in the Arnold Bennett vein, but with the light spicing of kedgeree. The recipe says 'serves 2' because it does, but I am not ashamed to say I snarfed the whole thing when I tested the recipe. It's lush.

1 knob (20–30 g/¾–1 oz) butter

5 cm (2 in) leek, thinly sliced

1 garlic clove, finely chopped

Place the butter in a medium bowl (I like plastic for this recipe because it releases the eggs well). Cook for about 30 seconds until melted, then stir in the leek and garlic. Cover and cook for 3 minutes.

100 ml (3½ fl oz/scant ½ cup) double (heavy) cream

1–2 teaspoons curry powder (to taste)

100–150 g (3½–5½ oz) smoked haddock, boneless and skinless

Add the cream and curry powder and mix well. Add the smoked haddock, whole, then cover and cook for another 3 minutes.

ⓒ

4 eggs

black pepper, to taste

30–40 g (1–1½ oz) medium Cheddar, sliced

a handful of coriander (cilantro) leaves and/or chives, roughly chopped

Tabasco or similar hot sauce, to taste

salt, to taste

Add the eggs to the bowl along with a few pinches of pepper, and beat lightly – I use a spatula or spoon rather than a whisk, to incorporate the cream through the whites while not breaking up the yolks or the fish too much. Crumble the cheese over the top of the egg mixture, cover and cook for 4 minutes–4 minutes 30 seconds, or until set but not too firm.

To serve, tip the omelette onto a plate and scatter with the coriander and/or chives. Splash on as much hot sauce as you like (but do use it – I think the richness really benefits from the heat and acidity). The omelette will probably be salty enough from the fish and cheese, but if not, season to taste with a little salt.

CHICKEN, RICE NOODLE AND BEAN SPROUT SALAD WITH SPICY SESAME PONZU

SERVES 4

Variations on this kind of salad – cold noodles, shredded chicken, crunchy veg, punchy dressing – have been a staple in my house for years. It's especially good on hot summer days, and using the microwave means you won't heat up your kitchen when you cook it.

2 chicken breasts, halved lengthways

1 tablespoon soy sauce

Combine the chicken breasts and soy sauce in a container, cover and cook for 5 minutes, tossing them once halfway through cooking. Check that the chicken is cooked through and, if not, toss again and keep cooking in 30-second intervals until done. Transfer to the refrigerator and leave to chill completely.

2 portions (about 100 g/3½ oz) rice vermicelli

Place the rice noodles in a bowl or container, add enough water to barely cover. Cover and cook for 4 minutes. Drain through a sieve (fine mesh strainer) and rinse well under cold water.

C

150 g (5½ oz) bean sprouts

½ cucumber, julienned

1 small-ish carrot, julienned or grated

1 small, spicy fresh chilli, finely sliced

1 tablespoon sesame seeds

a handful of fresh mint leaves, torn

9 tablespoons shop-bought ponzu, or 3 tablespoons each of sour citrus juice (lemon or lime), soy sauce and sugar

1 teaspoon sesame oil

chilli oil or hot chilli sauce (Sriracha or similar), to taste (optional)

Place the bean sprouts in a container (it can be the same one you used for the noodles), cover and cook for 3 minutes, then drain and rinse these under cold water as well. Keep everything in the refrigerator until ready to serve.

When the chicken (A) is nice and cold, shred it. Toss well with all of the remaining ingredients including the noodles (B) and bean sprouts.

HOT CHICKEN SANDWICH WITH YOGHURT MAYO

SERVES 2

Nashville hot chicken is one of America's most glorious culinary specialities – crisp and juicy fried chicken doused in a fire engine-red, blisteringly hot chilli oil. I can handle a lot of spice, but ordering the hottest chicken I could find when I was in Nashville turned out to be a painful mistake. A few bites in and I was a sweaty, hyperventilating mess, and by the time I was halfway through my meal the sensory overload began to warp my perception of space and time. The after-effects lasted 72 hours. Some people do drugs. Some people run marathons. I eat spicy chicken.

This is, of course, not a real Nashville hot chicken sandwich. It's not fried, and it lacks some other key components, too; particularly the buttermilk and pickle brine used to marinate the chicken. But it has some similarities, and if you don't hold back with the chilli, it will give you a similar kind of intense, sweaty, low-key hallucinatory eating experience.

A

½ tablespoon cayenne or similar hot chilli powder

1 teaspoon cornflour (cornstarch)

½ teaspoon smoked paprika

¼ teaspoon garlic granules

1 tablespoon vegetable oil

1 tablespoon soy sauce

1 teaspoon honey

Combine all these ingredients in a large bowl and stir well, ensuring there are no lumps of cornflour.

B

4 chicken skinless thigh fillets
(about 250 g/9 oz total)

Toss the chicken through the spice mixture, cover loosely and cook for 6 minutes, tossing the chicken twice throughout cooking.

1½ tablespoons Greek yoghurt

1½ tablespoons mayonnaise

2 burger buns, or 4 thick-cut slices of white bread, lightly toasted

6 leaves iceberg lettuce

6–8 slices of gherkin (dill pickle)

a big handful of salt and vinegar or dill crisps (chips), crushed

Meanwhile, stir together the yoghurt and mayo and spread a little of it on the bottom burger buns or bread. Lay a few leaves of iceberg lettuce on top of the buns, then lay the cooked chicken (B) on the lettuce, including the sauce (A) from the bowl. Top with the gherkins, crisps and the remaining yoghurt mayo, followed by the remaining bun/bread.

CHEESY CHICKEN BREASTS

SERVES 2

This recipe is one of my all-time favourites: simply chicken, cooked in a creamy tinned soup and white wine sauce, topped with Swiss cheese and croutons. I've been wanting to publish this recipe for ages, but somehow, never quite worked out how to justify it within the context of a Japanese cookbook. Both my grandma and my mom made it when I was a kid, and I *loved* it. How can you not love any recipe that starts with cream of chicken soup from a can? (Don't answer that.)

½ tin (150 ml/5 fl oz/scant ⅔ cup) of condensed cream of chicken soup

2 tablespoons white wine or dry vermouth

a pinch of grated nutmeg (optional)

a sprig of rosemary (optional)

a few grinds or shakes of black pepper

2 chicken breasts

40 g (1½ oz) Swiss cheese (such as Gruyère or Jarlsberg), grated

a big handful (about 30 g/1 oz) of shop-bought croutons

a few sprigs of parsley, chopped (optional)

Stir together the soup, wine, nutmeg, rosemary and pepper in a baking dish that fits the chicken fairly snugly (I used a 20 cm (8 in) round one). Add the chicken and toss it through the soup mixture, then top with the cheese, cover loosely and cook for 6 minutes. Scatter the croutons over the top, pressing them down slightly into the cheesy sauce, then cook, uncovered, for another minute. Garnish with the parsley (if using). Delicious with rice or bread, and some steamed green beans or asparagus.

GEKIKARA CHILLI CHICKEN RAMEN

SERVES 2

Ramen and curry shops in Japan often offer a variation on their product called *gekikara*, which roughly translates as 'extreme spice'. Inspired by this phenomenon, here's a spicy, one-pot ramen dish – the broth, the chicken and the noodles are all cooked in the same bowl. Whether or not you consider its heat level 'extreme' will depend on your tolerance for chilli, but it definitely has a kick!

3 spring onions (scallions), sliced

900 ml (30½ fl oz/3¾ cups) water

1 chicken leg, bone in but skin off

1 lemongrass stalk, split lengthways

4 tablespoons tahini

1 tablespoon miso (any kind)

1 tablespoon soy sauce, or more, to taste

2 tablespoons hot chilli oil

Divide the spring onions into white parts and green parts; set the green parts aside to use later. Combine the white parts with the water, chicken leg, lemongrass, tahini, miso, soy sauce and chilli oil in a large bowl, cover and cook for 20 minutes. Remove the lemongrass and discard, then take the chicken out and set on a board or plate to cool. When the chicken is cool enough to handle, shred it with your hands or forks into large chunks.

1 fresh hot chilli, finely sliced

2 garlic cloves, thinly sliced

150 g (5½ oz) dried ramen/egg noodles

½ pak choi (bok choi) or 1 baby pak choi, halved

100 g (3½ oz) bean sprouts

Add the fresh chilli and garlic to the broth (A) and whisk well to dissolve the miso and tahini. Add the noodles, pak choi and bean sprouts, cover and cook for 3–6 minutes until the noodles are done. Different noodles will absorb different amounts of water, so taste the broth and adjust the seasoning with more soy sauce as necessary.

2 tablespoons toasted sesame seeds, coarsely ground

a few big pinches of chilli (hot pepper) flakes

Transfer the noodles (B) to large bowls, then pour over the broth and top with the pak choi, bean sprouts (B) and shredded chicken (A). Garnish with the green parts of the spring onions, ground sesame and chilli flakes.

'BILL CLINTON' CHICKEN ORZO

SERVES 4

Why is this dish called 'Bill Clinton' chicken? I have absolutely no idea. When you Google it, page after page of enchilada recipes come up for some reason. (I gotcha covered, Bill – see page 133.) I asked my mom where it came from, as we used to eat it all the time growing up, and it appears in the family recipe book she made for my brother and me. Mom said it was originally a recipe submitted by Hillary Clinton in some regional American cookbook, but I can find no evidence of this either. Anyway, I guess it was one of Bill Clinton's favourite chicken recipes? We may never know. But it is easy to love – basically a lazy person's chicken Kiev, simply chicken cooked in an herby, garlicky butter. Orzo does not feature in the original recipe, but I love it because it soaks up all of the juices from the thighs, forming a substantial, risotto-like foundation to the dish, and makes it an all-in-one dinner. Serve it with something green on the side, or just chuck some frozen peas in to get your veg in.

200 g (7 oz) orzo

400 ml (13 fl oz/generous 1½ cups) water

40 g (1½ oz) butter

1 stock cube, crumbled (any kind, but chicken makes the most sense)

½ teaspoon each dried sage, marjoram, rosemary, thyme and pepper

¼ teaspoon salt

1 onion, finely chopped

2 garlic cloves, finely chopped

4 chicken thigh fillets

a few sprigs of parsley, chopped (optional)

Stir together all of the ingredients, except the chicken and parsley in a large bowl, then lay the chicken on top of the pasta. Cover and cook for 25 minutes. Stir before serving, and garnish with the chopped parsley (if using).

CHANGE IT UP!

Because of the amenable roast chickeny blandness of this dish, it takes well to a lot of different ingredients. Try it with a bit of chopped preserved lemon, cooked artichokes, sliced mushrooms, peas, asparagus, green beans or broccoli. Most of these should be added about two-thirds of the way through cooking so they don't overcook.

PORK FILLET WITH MISO, GINGER AND MARMALADE

SERVES 2–4

This recipe is originally based on one posted by the Japanese home cooking site *Macaroni*, an indispensable resource for microwave meals and other quick and simple dishes. It was a recipe for chashu – roasted or braised pork, commonly cooked for hours and enjoyed as a topping for ramen – but done in the microwave, in minutes. It sounded impossible, but it just looked so delicious that I had to try it.

It was a partial success, mainly because the cuts of pork we get here are not quite the same as they are in Japan. I used shoulder, which turned out okay, but the problem is that pork shoulder actually includes several different muscles; one of those muscles is very tough, and does not cook nicely in the microwave. So I switched to a cut which is more uniform – pork fillet – and it was great! Have this thinly sliced on a bowl of ramen, or simply with rice and some steamed greens (page 36) or fresh lettuce.

5 cm (2 in) leek (white part only)	Slice the leek into rounds, as thinly as you can. Keep in ice water (or in cold water in the refrigerator) until ready to serve for at least half an hour, which will make it more crisp and less harsh. Drain well and gently squeeze or pat dry before serving.

B

2 tablespoons miso (any kind)	In a large bowl, stir together the miso, marmalade, soy sauce, garlic, ginger and cornflour until no lumps of cornflour or miso remain, then pour in the water and mix well. Pierce the pork all over with a fork or a thin, sharp knife, and add it to the liquid. Cover the dish and cook for 4 minutes. Turn the pork, re-cover and cook for another 4 minutes, then let it rest in the bowl for 5–10 minutes. To serve, slice the pork thinly, pour over the sauce and garnish with the shredded leek (A). This can be enjoyed wrapped in lettuce leaves or with steamed rice, or both.
2 tablespoons marmalade	
2 tablespoons soy sauce	
1 garlic clove, grated	
2.5 cm (1 in) fresh ginger root, peeled and grated	
1 teaspoon cornflour (cornstarch)	
4 tablespoons water	
500 g (1 lb 2 oz) pork fillet	
lettuce leaves or steamed rice, to serve (optional)	

THREE-BEAN CHILLI CON HAM HOCK

SERVES 4

Generally speaking, I find vegetarian chilli just as satisfying as meaty chilli,
and this is indeed a *mostly* vegetarian recipe, but with some ham hock to add
little shreds of smoky salinity. You can leave it out, if you like – there's plenty
of flavour here without it.

50 g (1¾ oz) butter	Place the butter in a large bowl and cook, covered, for 1 minute until melted. Stir in the onion, celery and carrot, re-cover and cook for 8 minutes on power level 8, stirring halfway through cooking.
1 onion, diced	
2 celery stalks, diced	
1 carrot, diced	

10 g (½ oz) dried ancho chilli or similar, de-seeded and finely chopped (optional)	Add all of the spices and stir, then re-cover and cook on full power for 2 minutes.
1 tablespoon smoked paprika or chipotle powder	
1 teaspoon ground cumin	
1 teaspoon oregano	
1 teaspoon cocoa powder	
1 teaspoon garam masala (optional)	
1 teaspoon–1 tablespoon hot chilli powder (to taste)	
several grinds of black pepper	

1 × 400 g (14 oz) tin each of chickpeas (garbanzos), black beans and black-eyed peas, drained	Add all of the remaining ingredients and stir well, then re-cover and cook for 20 minutes, stirring halfway through cooking. Serve with rice, pasta or cornbread (page 55) and any of the garnishes you like.
1 × 400 g (14 oz) tin of finely chopped (crushed) tomatoes	
1 tablespoon tomato purée (paste)	
1 tablespoon ketchup	
1 tablespoon Bovril or Marmite	
100 g (3½ oz) shredded ham hock	
200 ml (7 fl oz/scant 1 cup) water	
salt or soy sauce, to taste	
lime wedges, sour cream, spring onions (scallions), jalapeños, toasted pumpkin seeds and coriander (cilantro) leaves, to garnish (all optional)	

PENNE WITH SAUSAGE AND PEPPERS

SERVES AT LEAST 3, POSSIBLY 4

One of my favourite easy meals is sausage and peppers, a simple, crowd-pleasing staple of Italian-American communities across the states, but particularly associated with Philadelphia. Add some pasta to this and you've got yourself a complete, delicious meal that cooks in the microwave in no time and in one dish.

200 g (7 oz) penne

1 tablespoon olive oil

4 garlic cloves, thinly sliced

1 teaspoon chilli (hot pepper) flakes

1 teaspoon dried oregano

250 ml (8 fl oz/1 cup) water

1 × 400 g (14 oz) tin of tomatoes (any kind)

60 g (2 oz) pitted green olives

2 (bell) peppers, de-seeded and roughly chopped (any kind)

300–400 g (10½–14 oz) sausages (fresh Italian fennel sausages are best, but any will do), pricked all over with a fork

a handful of basil or flat-leaf parsley leaves, torn or chopped

salt, to taste

grated Parmesan or similar, to garnish (optional)

Combine the penne, oil, garlic, chilli flakes, oregano, water and tomatoes in a large bowl and stir to mix. Add the olives, peppers and sausages on top. Cover and cook for 24 minutes, stirring every 8 minutes. Stir in the basil at the end of cooking, taste and adjust the seasoning with salt as you like (for me it usually doesn't need any). Garnish with grated Parmesan, if you like.

SPAGHETTI CARBONARA

SERVES 2

This is – genuinely – the most delicious carbonara I've ever made. The recipe itself doesn't really deviate from tradition – it's based on a very thorough and reassuringly no-nonsense one from the Italian food blog *Recipes From Italy*. It's mainly the cooking of the pasta and the method of emulsifying the sauce that's different; that's kind of what makes it so good. Because you're not dealing with a hot pan, there's very little risk of scrambling the eggs and the pasta cooks in the perfect amount of water to bind the sauce.

75 g (2½ oz) lardons (guanciale is the most traditional, but pancetta or bacon are fine!)	Combine the lardons with the oil in a large bowl. Stir well to coat and cook, uncovered, for 2 minutes 30 seconds, stirring a couple times throughout cooking to break them up. Leave in the bowl to cool; don't discard the rendered fat.
1 teaspoon olive or vegetable oil	

200 g (7 oz) spaghetti	In a separate container, combine the spaghetti with the water and a spoonful of the fat from the rendered lardons (A). Stir, cover and cook for 12 minutes, stirring again halfway through cooking.
450 ml (15 fl oz/scant 2 cups) water	

2 eggs	Meanwhile, when the lardons and their fat (A) have cooled, tip the eggs, cheese and pepper into the bowl, whisking well so the egg is beaten.
50 g (1¾ oz) pecorino (or similar), finely grated, plus extra to serve if desired	
lots of black pepper	

When the pasta is done cooking, remove the cover and stir it in its container to break up any clumps (it won't be stuck together, but it needs to be loosened up before adding to the sauce). Tip the cooked pasta along with any remaining pasta water (there won't be much) into the egg mixture, and toss well using tongs, so the spaghetti is well coated. Serve immediately. If you like, you can garnish with more pecorino and pepper (but for me this is not necessary).

NOTE If you don't have something that fits the spaghetti whole, you'll have to either break up the pasta so it fits better, or stir it a few times at the beginning of cooking as it softens until it all fits in the container you're using, submerged in the water. If this seems like too much of a faff – and to be honest, it is – you can try this with a different pasta shape that fits better in the bowl.

LAMB, POTATO AND AUBERGINE CASSEROLE

SERVES 4

If you read that recipe title and thought, 'oh, it's a moussaka,' you would be … sort of right. Likewise, if you thought, 'oh, it's a Lancashire hotpot, but which someone decided to ruin by adding aubergine (eggplant),' you would again be mostly right. This recipe was inspired by both dishes, but the end result – while delicious – would not be accepted as moussaka by any Greek nor as Lancashire hotpot by any Northerner. Still, the combination of lamb, potato and aubergine in pretty much any form is undeniably comforting, especially when blanketed in an (optional) cheese-seasoned white sauce. You will need a 3 litre (101 fl oz/12 cup) bowl for this recipe.

2 aubergines (eggplants), ends cut off and cut into long, wide planks, about 1 cm (½ in) thick and 2.5 cm (1 in) across

250 g (9 oz) potatoes, washed (no need to peel) and cut into chip-like batons

3 tablespoons olive oil

250 g (9 oz) minced (ground) lamb

250 g (9 oz) Cumberland sausage meat (or similar)

¼ teaspoon salt

black pepper, to taste

3 garlic cloves, thinly sliced

1 tablespoon dried oregano

a few sprigs of flat-leaf parsley, finely chopped and thyme, leaves picked

½ teaspoon ground cinnamon

1 × 400 g (14 oz) tin of chopped or crushed tomatoes

2 tablespoons tomato purée (paste)

80 g (2¾ oz) pitted green or kalamata olives

Toss the aubergines and potatoes with the oil and place in a baking dish. Cover and cook for 3 minutes, then uncover, toss and cook for another 3 minutes. Combine all the remaining ingredients and mix well, then tip this into the baking dish and stir through the aubergine and potatoes. Cover and cook for 15 minutes, then uncover, stir and cook for another 15 minutes.

You can serve this on its own, as is, and it will be perfectly tasty. But if you fancy gilding the lily, proceed with the recipe to make the white sauce.

30 g (1 oz) butter

30 g (1 oz/¼ cup) plain (all-purpose) flour

200 ml (7 fl oz/scant 1 cup) milk

1 egg

30 g (1 oz) pecorino or similar cheese, finely grated

3 tablespoons plain yoghurt

salt and white pepper, to taste

Combine the butter and flour in a large bowl and cook, covered, for 30 seconds, so the butter melts. Whisk the butter and flour together to make a smooth paste, then add a little splash of the milk to loosen the paste, then the rest of the milk, little by little, whisking as you go. Beat in the egg and cheese, ensuring the egg is well mixed into the milk. Cover and cook for 4 minutes, whisking after every minute, being careful to scrape down the sides and bottom of the bowl to prevent clumping. When the sauce is thickened, whisk in the yoghurt, taste and adjust the seasoning with salt and pepper as necessary. To serve, the white sauce can be poured over the casserole (A) and re-heated together, or it can simply be served on the side.

VENISON AND BACON COTTAGE PIE

SERVES 4

I made this with venison because it was on offer, but you could use any minced (ground) meat you like. The real star of the show here is the copious amounts of bacon, which adds an incredibly moreish saltiness and light smokiness to what is otherwise a fairly standard cottage pie.

A

600–650 g (1 lb 5 oz–1 lb 7 oz) potatoes, peeled and cut into 2.5 cm (1 in) chunks

10 whole garlic cloves, peeled, with bottoms trimmed off

30 g (1 oz) butter

¼ teaspoon salt (or a little more, to taste)

4 tablespoons milk

a few shakes of white pepper (optional)

Combine the potatoes and garlic in a medium baking dish (I used a 23 cm (9 in) round one) with a splash of water. Cover and cook for 12 minutes, stirring twice during cooking, until mashably soft. Tip into a separate bowl and add the butter and mash well, then mash in the salt, milk and white pepper (if using).

B

1 tablespoon olive oil

100 g (3½ oz) bacon lardons

2 banana shallots or 1 onion, finely chopped

½ teaspoon caraway seeds (optional)

1 pinch of dried rosemary (optional)

black pepper, to taste

1 carrot, grated

1 celery stalk, finely chopped

4 button or chestnut mushrooms, grated

300 g (10½ oz) minced (ground) venison

Wipe out the baking dish and add the oil, lardons and shallots or onion. Stir well so everything is coated in the oil. Cook, uncovered, for 4 minutes, then stir in the caraway and rosemary (if using) along with the black pepper, carrot, celery and mushrooms. Cook for another 4 minutes. Add the minced venison and break it up with a fork, working it through the vegetable and bacon mixture, and cook for another 4 minutes.

C

150 ml (5 fl oz/scant ⅔ cup) brown stock (beef, chicken or mushroom)

1 tablespoon Worcestershire sauce

1 tablespoon tomato purée (paste)

1 teaspoon cornflour (cornstarch)

4–5 sprigs of thyme

100 g (3½ oz) peas

Stir together the stock, Worcestershire sauce, tomato purée and cornflour so there are no lumps of cornflour, then tip this into the venison mixture (B). Add the thyme, mix well and break up any big clumps of venison, cover and cook for 8 minutes. Stir in the peas, then top with the mash (A). At this point, you can cook the whole thing straight away – it will take just a few more minutes, uncovered, to warm through. But you can also put it in the refrigerator and cook it from chilled, in which case you should cook it for about 8 minutes, covered, to ensure even and thorough heating.

MEATBALL SUBS

SERVES 4

Meatball subs are great because they allow you to forgo the dainty pretence of cutlery and eat meatballs with your hands. Remember that scene in *The Wedding Singer* where the old lady pays Adam Sandler's character for piano lessons with meatballs, and she scoops them directly into his hands? I love that scene. I believe there's something more satisfying about food when you can sink your teeth directly into it, rather than having it cut up beforehand. Anyhoo, if you wish, these meatballs in sauce don't have to go into subs – they're perfectly tasty on pasta.

A

---

750 g (1 lb 10 oz) minced (ground) meat – I like 50/50 pork and beef, but use whatever you like

40 g (1½ oz) grated Parmesan or similar

1½ tablespoons fennel seeds

1 egg

6 garlic cloves, minced, or 2 tablespoons garlic purée

3 tablespoons breadcrumbs

1½ tablespoons arrowroot (optional, but it helps make the meatballs super soft)

1 tablespoon dried oregano

1 tablespoon dried marjoram

½ teaspoon salt

black pepper, as much as you like

Thoroughly mix all ingredients and form into 12 balls.

B

2 tablespoons olive oil

9 garlic cloves, minced, or 3 tablespoons garlic purée

1 onion, finely chopped

1 tablespoon dried oregano

50 g (1¾ oz) tomato purée (paste)

2 × 400 g (14 oz) tins of crushed tomatoes or 800 g passata

20 g (¾ oz) basil leaves, roughly chopped

1 tablespoon ketchup

¼ teaspoon salt

black pepper and/or chilli (hot pepper) flakes, to taste

Combine the oil, garlic and onion in a deep bowl, cover and cook for 5 minutes, stirring halfway. Add the oregano, tomato purée and tinned tomatoes, cover and cook for 20 minutes, stirring halfway. At the end, stir in the chopped basil, ketchup, salt and pepper or chilli, taste and adjust the seasoning as needed.

C

4 sturdy sub rolls

8 slices provolone or similar mild, melty cheese

pickled jalapeños and/or sliced green olives, to taste (optional)

Place the balls (A) in a baking dish and pour over the sauce (B), tossing them to coat. Cover and cook for 15 minutes, turning the balls over and moving them around the dish halfway through cooking. Cut the rolls open and lay the cheese slices on the bottom. Spoon the meatballs into the rolls and garnish with the jalapeños and/or green olives, if you like. Enjoy piping hot, before the bread falls apart!

IMAGE OVERLEAF →

CHORIZO, MUSHROOM, OLIVE AND FENNEL SEED FRITTATA

SERVES 2–4

This isn't really a frittata, I guess – 'frittata' means 'fried', so this is a … microwattata?!
No idea. Anyway, it's microwaved eggs, studded with some of my favourite pizza
toppings. So it's like an eggy pizza quiche thing. Sorry, I am not selling this well!
Just try it, I promise it's delicious, and an incredibly quick and easy dish that can
be breakfast, lunch or dinner – and decent picnic fodder, too.

250 g (9 oz) cooking chorizo, skin removed
and broken into small crumbles

1 teaspoon fennel seeds

150 g (5½ oz) white or chestnut mushrooms, sliced

50 g (1¾ oz) green olives, sliced

6 eggs, beaten

25–30 g (¾–1 oz) Parmesan, grana Padano or similar
hard cheese, sliced

a few sprigs of flat-leaf parsley leaves, chopped

black pepper, to taste

a drizzle of tasty olive oil (optional)

Mix the chorizo and fennel seeds in a large
bowl and cook for 2 minutes, then stir in the
mushrooms and cook for another 3 minutes.
Add the olives, beaten eggs and cheese and mix
well, then cover and cook for 6 minutes. Garnish
with the parsley, black pepper and a drizzle of oil,
if using. Cut into wedges to serve.

REFRIGERATOR/FREEZER CLEAR-OUT JAPANESE CURRY

SERVES 4

This isn't so much a recipe as it is a guide for using up odds and ends in your refrigerator or freezer to make a quick Japanese curry rice. Japanese curry (or 'katsu curry', as it is perhaps more commonly but erroneously known) is mellow enough to take pretty much any vegetable or protein. This makes it great to have on hand for easy, crowd-pleasing dinners. The roux cooks beautifully in the microwave, too. Unlike cooking on the hob, it dissolves evenly and won't stick to the bottom of the pan.

meat and veg from your refrigerator or freezer – whatever you have

1 pack of Japanese curry roux (90–100 g/3¼–3½ oz)

rice, to serve (see cooking method on page 31, or just cook the rice however you like)

If you have any hard, fresh veg, such as potatoes, carrots, baby corn or cauliflower, cook these first, by themselves – there is a general guide to steaming veg on page 36. Once cooked to your liking, set them aside. If you're using fresh raw meat, cut it into bite-size pieces. (Don't use frozen raw meat – defrost it first.)

Break up the curry roux into small pieces and place them in a large bowl. Check the pack instructions and add about 20 per cent less water than it says to use – the ingredients you add, especially frozen ones, will release water into the sauce, so you need to compensate for that. (You can thin the curry out with more water at the end if it's too thick, but you can't really reduce it if it's too thin.)

Cover the bowl and cook for 6 minutes, stirring halfway through until the roux dissolves and the mixture boils. At this point, add the raw meat (if using), re-cover and cook for at least 4 minutes until the mixture boils again and the meat is cooked through. If you're using frozen veg, stir it in, cover and cook again until the mixture boils – how long will depend on how much veg you add, but bank on at least 3 minutes, probably more like 6. At the very end, stir in any cooked fresh veg you may have and heat briefly so everything is piping hot. Serve with cooked rice, ideally Japanese white rice.

RICH GARLIC
AND MUSHROOM RAGÙ

SERVES 4

Microwaving mushrooms causes them to expel moisture, essentially creating a rich mushroom broth in an instant. This recipe harnesses that to make a killer sauce that can be enjoyed on pasta, polenta, ancient grains, good crusty bread ... whatever carb you like, really!

Ⓐ

2 garlic bulbs

Microwave the garlic bulbs, unpeeled, for 30 seconds. This will cause them to soften slightly and make them easy to peel.

Ⓑ

½ onion, finely chopped

4 tablespoons olive oil

600 g (1 lb 5 oz) white mushrooms, very thinly sliced

2 tablespoons wine (any kind)

1 tablespoon dried oregano

1 tablespoon soy sauce

several grinds of black pepper

Peel each garlic clove (A) and place in a large bowl along with the onion and oil and stir well. Cook for 3 minutes, stirring halfway through cooking, then roughly mash the garlic with a fork. Add the mushrooms, wine, oregano, soy sauce and pepper and mix well, then cook, uncovered, for 10 minutes, stirring halfway through cooking.

Ⓒ

1 tablespoon tomato purée (paste)

1 × 400 g (14 oz) tin of tomatoes (any kind)

a handful of basil and/or flat-leaf parsley leaves

salt, to taste

Add the tomato purée and tinned tomatoes, stir well and cook for another 10 minutes. Then stir and continue to cook for another 5–10 minutes until the sauce has reduced and thickened to your liking. (I like a very rich, jammy sauce, so I cook it for the full 10 minutes.) When it's done, stir through some torn basil and/or parsley, taste and add salt as needed.

SAAG PANEER

SERVES 4

My original head chef at the restaurant was one Rivaaj Maharaj, still one of the most talented chefs and all-around best dudes I know. Though Rivaaj was certainly a dab hand at making ramen – and his hot chicken wings are other-worldly – his background is in South African Indian food, and over the years he's shared his knowledge of that cuisine quite generously with me. One of the more interesting tips I've learned from him is to make saag paneer with tinned greens called *sarson ka saag*, which contain mustard greens and seasonings in addition to just the usual spinach. As sarson ka saag is not that easy to come by, this recipe uses ordinary tinned spinach instead, bolstered with a foundation of aromatic spices and onions.

1 onion, diced	Combine the onion, garlic, ginger, cumin, mustard seeds and butter or ghee in a large bowl. Cover and cook for 4 minutes, stirring halfway through cooking. Stir in the chilli and methi leaves (if using), re-cover and cook for another 2 minutes.
2 garlic cloves, finely chopped	
2.5 cm (1 in) fresh ginger root, peeled and finely chopped	
1 teaspoon cumin seeds	
1 teaspoon black mustard seeds	
4 tablespoons butter or ghee	
1 red chilli, split lengthways (optional)	
4 tablespoons dried methi leaves (optional)	

800 g (1 lb 12 oz) tinned chopped spinach	Add the tinned spinach, paneer and stock cube, stir well, loosely cover and cook for 10 minutes, stirring halfway through cooking. Stir, taste and adjust the seasoning as you like with chilli powder and salt. Serve with rice or parathas.
400 g (14 oz) paneer, cut into 2.5 cm (1 in) cubes	
1 stock cube, crumbled (any kind)	
chilli powder, to taste (optional)	
salt, to taste	
rice or parathas, to serve	

RIGATONI ALLA GIN MARTINI

SERVES 2—3

Vodka sauce is delicious, but what exactly is the point of the vodka? I've read that if you add the right amount at the right time, it makes the tomato sauce taste sweeter and more aromatic. Maybe that's true ... but I still think the vodka would be put to better use by, you know, drinking it. However! What if we replaced the vodka with something more flavourful? I often cook with vermouth anyway, so it's not too much of a leap to cook with gin as well. And if we're cooking with gin and vermouth, we may as well chuck the whole martini in there and add olives. So here it is: a riff on the classic rigatoni alla vodka with a bit more going on, flavour-wise.

Ⓐ

200 g (7 oz) rigatoni or similar tubular pasta

500 g (1 lb 2 oz) passata or tinned chopped tomatoes

100 ml (3½ fl oz/scant ½ cup) water

80 g (2¾ oz) pitted green olives

50 g (1¾ oz) tomato purée (paste)

2 garlic cloves, minced or grated

1 tablespoon olive oil

Combine everything in a large bowl, cover and cook for 12 minutes.

Ⓑ

6 tablespoons white vermouth

1 pinch each of chilli (hot pepper) flakes and dried oregano

Add the vermouth, chilli and oregano, stir well, re-cover and cook for 8 minutes.

100 ml (3½ fl oz/scant ½ cup) double (heavy) cream

1 tablespoon olive brine

20–30 g (¾–1½ oz) Parmesan, finely grated, plus more to garnish

salt and black pepper, to taste

gin, to taste

Stir in the cream and olive brine and cook, uncovered, for 2 minutes. Stir in the Parmesan, taste and adjust the seasoning with salt and black pepper. Add a few drops of gin at the very end – I do this by putting my thumb over the top of the gin bottle and shaking it over the pasta. Stir well and serve with extra Parmesan and black pepper on top.

CHANGE IT UP!

This is a pretty versatile sauce and can take a variety of other protein or veg additions. Some suggestions:

SAUSAGE OR CHICKEN

These can be added raw, in small pieces, halfway through cooking the pasta.

PRAWNS (SHRIMP)

Add these towards the end of cooking (with about 5 minutes left).

MUSHROOMS OR COURGETTES (ZUCCHINI)

Slice them thickly and add halfway through cooking; reduce the water in the recipe to 60 ml (2 fl oz/¼ cup) to account for the added liquid these will release.

CAPONATA

Caponata, the Sicilian stew/relish based mainly on aubergines (eggplants) and olives, is one of my all-time favourite home-cooked dishes. It's wildly flavourful, with its seasonings of capers, vinegar and sugar; it's good hot or cold; it works well with pasta, polenta, wholegrains or bread; and it's a delicious way to get quite a lot of veg in. And it turns out it cooks pretty well in the microwave, too.

It should be noted that this recipe should not be taken as representative of real Sicilian caponata, as it varies from the original in a number of ways – such as the inclusion of fennel instead of onion, and the fact that the vegetables are simply stewed rather than par-fried first ... and also, you know, it's cooked in the microwave. Still, this is a very tasty, very versatile dish – hence the relatively large batch size. You'll get through it! You will need a 3 litre (101 fl oz/12 cup) bowl for this recipe.

A

2 aubergines (eggplants), de-stemmed, cut into quarters and then into wedges about 2 cm (¾ in) thick

6 celery stalks, roughly chopped

1 fennel bulb, thinly sliced

10 garlic cloves (1 bulb's worth), roots removed and peeled

1 red (bell) pepper, de-seeded and roughly chopped

6 tablespoons olive oil

Toss all of the fresh vegetables with the oil in a large bowl, cover and cook for 10 minutes.

B

2 × 400 g (14 oz) tins of peeled plum tomatoes

1 tablespoon dried oregano

100 g (3½ oz) pitted olives (I like kalamata for this, but green olives are good, too)

60 g (2 oz) capers (baby capers)

Add all of the ingredients, mix well and cook, covered, for 20 minutes, then stir well and cook for another 20 minutes, uncovered.

1 tablespoon red wine vinegar

1 tablespoon caster (superfine) sugar

chilli (hot pepper) flakes, to taste (optional)

a small handful of flat-leaf parsley or basil leaves, finely chopped

Stir in the vinegar, sugar and a pinch or two of chilli, if you like, and cook for another 5 minutes until the mixture is thick and jammy. Leave to cool slightly, then stir in the fresh herbs. This can be enjoyed hot and fresh, but I think it is better after spending a night in the refrigerator. Personally I like it better cold than hot!

JACKFRUIT AND MUSHROOM ENCHILADAS

SERVES 2, GENEROUSLY, ON ITS OWN, AND UP TO 4 WITH A SIDE OR TWO

Here's a thing I didn't know: 'enchilada' is a conjugation of 'enchilar', a Spanish verb meaning 'to add chilli to' – so enchilada literally means 'seasoned with chilli'. I love this verb and I wish we had an English equivalent. Anyway, this is a pretty good vegetarian enchilada recipe using jackfruit and mushrooms to provide a meaty, savoury, pleasantly fibrous filling, using shop-bought salsas as a shortcut.

150 g (5½ oz) oyster mushrooms or similar meaty, fibrous mushrooms, sliced

200 g (7 oz) tinned green jackfruit (drained weight)

1 tablespoon soy sauce

1 teaspoon smoked paprika

1 teaspoon cocoa powder

½ teaspoon ground cumin

1 tablespoon tomato purée (paste)

½ teaspoon brown sugar (any kind)

salt, to taste

Combine the mushrooms, jackfruit, soy sauce, paprika, cocoa and cumin in a bowl and cook, uncovered, for 8 minutes, stirring halfway through cooking. Add the tomato purée and sugar, stir well and cook for another 4 minutes. Taste and adjust the seasoning as you like with salt, but err on the side of caution as this will be topped with salsas and cheese that may be quite salty.

10 small (12 cm/5 in) corn tortillas

Fill each tortilla with a big spoonful of the mushroom mixture (A). Roll them up like little cigars, then arrange them in rows in a baking dish (I use one which is 18 × 23 cm (7 × 9 in) and they fit perfectly in a 5 × 2 arrangement).

C

100 g (3½ oz) tomatillo salsa or similar tart, green salsa

100 g (3½ oz) chipotle in adobo or similar rich, spicy red salsa

50–60 g (1¾–2 oz/scant ¼–¼ cup) sour cream

120 g (4½ oz) grated mild Cheddar

Cover the tortillas (B) with stripes of green and red salsa and dollops of sour cream, then with the grated cheese. Cook, uncovered, for 12–15 minutes, until the cheese is melted and the filling is piping hot.

SWE

ETS

CITRUS CURD WITH PASSION FRUIT PASTRY CREAM

MAKES 4 BIG PUDS, OR 8 LITTLE ONES

Jay Rayner, one of the UK's most influential food critics and jazz pianists –
who I am also honoured to call a friend – wrote a thing a few years ago lamenting
the replacement of proper desserts on restaurant menus with 'creamy things
chucked in a bowl'. I'm typically in agreement with Jay's opinions, but not this time.
I love me a creamy thing in a bowl. And if I ever get invited around to Jay's house
(I probably won't), I'm going to bring this pudding over to argue my case.

100 g (3½ oz) butter

200 g (7 oz/scant 1 cup) caster (superfine) sugar

juice and zest from 1 grapefruit, 2 lemons and 2 limes

4 eggs, plus 4 egg yolks

Place the butter in a medium bowl and cook for 30 seconds, covered, until melted. Whisk in the sugar and citrus juice and zest, then the eggs and egg yolks, whisking well so they are evenly beaten. Cook, uncovered, for 3 minutes, whisking well halfway through cooking and again at the end. Keep cooking in 30-second bursts, whisking after each one, until the mixture is thick. (This will take about 5 minutes total, including the initial 3-minute cook.) Pass the curd through a sieve (fine mesh strainer), cover and chill in the refrigerator until ready to serve.

1 teaspoon vanilla extract or paste

60 g (2 oz/¼ cup) sugar

2 egg yolks

10 g (½ oz/1½ tablespoons) cornflour (cornstarch)

7 g (¼ oz/1 tablespoon) plain (all-purpose) flour

240 ml (8 fl oz/1 cup) milk

pulp and seeds from 2 passion fruits

100 ml (3½ fl oz/scant ½ cup) double (heavy) or whipping cream

Whisk together the vanilla, sugar, yolks and flours in a medium bowl to make a coarse paste. Whisk in a splash of milk, to thin the yolk mixture, then the rest of it, little by little, until smooth. Cook, uncovered, for 4 minutes, whisking well after each minute. By now the pastry cream should be very thick, but if not, keep cooking in 30-second increments, whisking each time, until it is. Stir in the passion fruit pulp and seeds and cover with a piece of cling film (plastic wrap) or parchment placed directly on the surface of the custard. Leave to cool to room temperature, then transfer to the refrigerator to chill completely. When the custard is cold, whip the cream in a separate bowl to soft peaks, then fold in the chilled pastry cream.

4–8 custard creams or wafer rolls

Spoon some curd (A) into glasses or dessert bowls, then spoon the pastry cream (B) on top. Decorate each one with a biscuit (cookie).

MISO WALNUT BROWNIES

MAKES 12–16 BROWNIES

Walnuts are fairly far down the list in my nut power rankings (it goes: macadamia, pecan, peanut, pistachio, hazelnut, pine nut, Brazil nut, walnut, cashew, almond) but I do like them in brownies. Miso has an affinity with both walnuts and chocolate, adding a nice fruitiness and, of course, saltiness to the mix. But if you don't have miso, feel free to leave it out – just replace it with 1 teaspoon salt and the recipe will work the same.

180 g (6½ oz) butter
200 g (7 oz) dark chocolate, chopped
100 g (3½ oz) milk chocolate, chopped
60–80 g (2–2¾ oz) miso (use more for a stronger, saltier flavour) (any kind)
320 g (11 oz/1¾ cups) light brown sugar

Combine the butter and chocolates in a large bowl and cook, covered, for 2 minutes until completely melted, stirring with a spatula at the end of cooking to ensure the mixture is smooth. Whisk in the miso, then the sugar.

4 eggs
1 teaspoon vanilla extract
180 g (6½ oz/1½ cups) plain (all-purpose) flour
50 g (1¾ oz) cocoa powder
1 teaspoon baking powder
80 g (2¾ oz/generous ¾ cups) walnuts, roughly chopped

Beat the eggs into the chocolate mixture (A), one by one, whisking hard until the mixture is smooth and glossy. Add the vanilla, then the flour, cocoa powder and baking powder. Mix well with a whisk, then a spatula, to scrape down the sides and bottom of the bowl and fully incorporate the liquid into the dry ingredients. Finally, stir in the walnuts. Tip into a 23 × 23 cm (9 × 9 in) silicone baking dish, then cover and cook for 10–12 minutes. Cool completely before slicing and serving.

AUNT NOËL'S BANANA CAKE WITH CHOCOLATE GANACHE AND TOASTED NUTS

SERVES 9—16

Everybody loves my sister-in-law Noël's banana bread. What makes it so good?
Well, it's basically a cake, considering how much sugar and butter is in it. Noël serves
it as a side dish at Thanksgiving, but frankly this has always struck me as quite weird.
Banana and turkey? I'm imagining her trying to serve this on *MasterChef*. John
and Gregg would utterly deplete their arsenal of incredulous facial expressions.
But anyway it's a delicious cake, especially with sweet chocolate and
crunchy nuts on top.

4 bananas	The bananas here should be very, very ripe – totally brown and soft. If they're not, you can 'ripen' them in the microwave by cooking them in their peels for 1–2 minutes until they soften. Leave them to cool before proceeding with the recipe.
100 g (3½ oz/scant ½ cup) caster (superfine) sugar	
150 g (5½ oz/¾ cup) dark brown sugar	
120 g (4½ oz) butter, at room temperature, plus a little more, for greasing	Beat the sugars and butter together until smooth, then add the bananas and mash well. Beat in the eggs, then the buttermilk/yoghurt and vanilla. Beat in the remaining ingredients, using a spatula to scrape down the sides of the bowl until the batter just comes together. Tip into a lightly buttered, deep baking dish (23 cm (9 in) diameter or about 20 cm (8 in) square), ideally silicone, but any material will do. Cook, uncovered, for 8–10 minutes, then cover and cook for another 4–5 minutes, or until the middle of the cake sets. Leave to cool in the dish before serving.
2 eggs	
120 ml (4 fl oz/½ cup) buttermilk or plain yoghurt	
1 teaspoon vanilla extract	
250 g (9 oz/2 cups) plain (all-purpose) flour	
1 teaspoon bicarbonate of soda (baking soda)	
½ teaspoon baking powder	
¼ teaspoon salt	

100 g (3½ oz/¾ cups) macadamia nuts	Tip the macadamia nuts out onto a plate and toss them with the oil and salt so they are evenly coated. Microwave on power level 7 for 2 minutes, then stir them around the plate and repeat this process twice more, until the nuts are aromatic (6 minutes in total). Note that the microwave has the unusual effect of toasting the *inside* of the nuts before their outsides take on colour, so use your nose rather than your eyes for this. Leave to cool completely, then coarsely chop.
½ teaspoon vegetable oil	
a pinch of salt	

1 quantity chocolate ganache (page 151)	Follow the instructions on page 151. Pour the ganache over the cake and sprinkle on the chopped nuts (B). Leave to cool completely before serving.

OVERNIGHT CINNAMON ROLLS

MAKES 9 ROLLS

Overnight oats are nice, aren't they? You stir some oats up with some other stuff, you put in the refrigerator and in the morning you've got … cold porridge, I guess? Hooray. As delightful as that is, I have an alternative to offer: hot and fresh cinnamon rolls. You can make these in the evening, then leave them to slowly prove in the refrigerator, and in the morning you whack 'em in the microwave and they're ready in 8 minutes. And the best thing about these is that because there's no dry heat in the microwave, the cinnamon rolls come out soft and squishy throughout, with no hard edges. They're basically cinnamon rolls where the entire roll is the gooey middle – an absolute win, in my book.

50 g (1¾ oz) butter

150 ml (5 fl oz/scant ⅔ cup) milk

1 packet (7 g/¼ oz) dried yeast

2 tablespoons light brown sugar

¼ teaspoon salt

300 g (10½ oz/scant 2½ cups) plain (all-purpose) flour, plus more for dusting

Place the butter and milk in a mixing bowl and cook, uncovered, for 30 seconds–1 minute, to melt the butter and gently warm the milk. Feel the mixture with your finger – if it's really hot, let it cool to body temperature before proceeding. Whisk in the yeast and sugar until both dissolve, then stir in the salt and flour until a sticky dough forms. Set aside while you make the filling.

60 g (2 oz) butter

80 g (2¾ oz/scant ½ cup) dark brown sugar

1 tablespoon ground cinnamon

If the butter is cold, cook it for 10 seconds or so until it softens, then beat in the sugar and cinnamon.

Dust your counter with plenty of flour and tip the dough out onto it. Roll the dough (A) out into a rectangle about 25 × 40 cm (10 × 16 in), then spread the cinnamon filling all over the dough, leaving about 1 cm (½ in) of naked dough along the outside. Roll the rectangle up into a log, then cut the log into nine spirals. Place the spirals into a 23 × 23 cm (9 × 9 in) glass or silicone baking dish, cover with cling film (plastic wrap) and leave in the refrigerator to slowly rise overnight.

120 g (4½ oz/1 cup) icing (powdered) sugar

1 tablespoon warm water

½ teaspoon vanilla (optional)

To make the icing, mix everything together to form a thick glaze.

With the cover still on the rolls, cook them for 8 minutes. Leave to cool slightly before pouring on the glaze, then leave the glaze to set. Enjoy warm and fresh.

CINNAMON ROLL RULES

1. The best cinnamon roll is the one that appears at the moment you need it most.

2. Doughiness is next to godliness. Texture is overrated.

3. Two wrongs don't make a right, but two cinnamon rolls usually do.

4. Cinnamon rolls are not a breakfast item, they are a dessert that is eaten at breakfast time (this is an important distinction).

EMERGENCY MIXING BOWL COOKIE CAKE

SERVES 1–3

Edd Kimber's 'emergency chocolate chip cookie', from his book *Small Batch Bakes,* is a work of brilliance: a single-serving cookie recipe using simple storecupboard ingredients, ready to eat in under 20 minutes. This recipe takes that concept and makes it even faster through the power of microwave cooking – done in (no joke) around 5 minutes. The inclusion of nuts and/or cereal comes from one of my favourite childhood cookies – ranger cookies – and adds interesting textural bits to the otherwise soft, gooey cookie.

NOTE This recipe calls for ¹⁄₁₆ teaspoon each of baking powder and bicarbonate of soda (baking soda). I don't actually expect you to have a ¹⁄₁₆ teaspoon – just use a ¼ or ⅛ teaspoon and eyeball it.

2 tablespoons butter	Combine the butter and milk in a pasta bowl or similar shallow dish and cook for 30 seconds so the butter melts and the milk warms up.
2 tablespoons milk	

4 tablespoons light brown sugar	Whisk in the sugar, then add all of the remaining ingredients except the chocolate and ice cream, and mix well. Fold in the chocolate chunks, tidy the edges of the bowl with a cloth or paper towel, then cook, uncovered for 1 minute–1 minute 30 seconds. Leave to cool for 1–2 minutes, then enjoy straight from the bowl, with a scoop or two of ice cream on top.
6 tablespoons plain (all-purpose) flour	
⅛ teaspoon vanilla extract (optional)	
4 tablespoons breakfast cereal, desiccated (dried shredded) coconut, flaked (slivered) almonds, chopped pistachios or similar – or a mix of several	
¹⁄₁₆ teaspoon baking powder	
¹⁄₁₆ teaspoon bicarbonate of soda (baking soda)	
a pinch of salt	
2 tablespoons chocolate chips or chunks, milk or dark or a mix of both	
ice cream, as needed	

GRAPEFRUIT AND HONEY MIXING BOWL DRIZZLE CAKE

SERVES 8—10

I absolutely love the aroma of fresh grapefruit – it's almost impossible not to feel uplifted when you slice into one. This cake captures all the zingy juice and oils from the fruit beautifully, and it has the added benefit of being cooked in the same bowl you mix it in.

1 pink grapefruit	For best results, have everything at room temperature before you begin. Zest the grapefruit and one of the lemons with a fine grater, then squeeze their juices into a medium-sized bowl, catching any seeds with your hands or a sieve (fine mesh strainer). Add about a third of the zest to the juice along with the honey. Cook, uncovered, for 2–3 minutes until the mixture boils and infuses. Set aside while you prepare the cake.
2 lemons	
100 g (3½ oz/scant ⅓ cup) honey	

200 g (7 oz) butter	Place the butter in a large plastic bowl and cook, uncovered, for 1 minute on power level 5 so it becomes very soft (it's okay if it melts a bit). Tip in the honey along with the sugar and whisk hard for a few minutes until the mixture is light and smooth. Beat in the eggs, one at a time, until well mixed, then add the flour, cornmeal, bicarbonate of soda, baking powder and salt. Mix until just combined, then fold in the remaining citrus zest with a spatula, scraping down the sides and bottom of the bowl as you go. Cover the bowl and cook for 6 minutes. While the cake is still warm, stab it repeatedly with a thin chopstick or skewer, then pour over half of the citrus-honey syrup (A). Return to the microwave and cook, uncovered, for 1 minute. Leave to cool, then turn the cake out of the bowl and onto a plate. Stab holes in the upper surface of the cake as you did with the bottom, and pour over the rest of the grapefruit drizzle.
50 g (1¾ oz/2 tablespoons) honey	
150 g (5½ oz/¾ cup) caster (superfine) sugar, ideally golden	
3 eggs	
200 g (7 oz/1⅔ cups) plain (all-purpose) flour	
50 g (⅓ cup) fine cornmeal (or polenta)	
1 teaspoon bicarbonate of soda (baking soda)	
1½ teaspoons baking powder	
¼ teaspoon salt	

120 g (4½ oz/1 cup) icing (powdered) sugar	Stir together the icing sugar, lemon juice and food colouring to make a drizzle-able pink icing, then pour this all over the cake and finish with a liberal scattering of sprinkles. Let the icing set before serving.
1 tablespoon lemon juice	
pink or red food colouring, as needed	
sprinkles, as needed	

TRIPLE CHOCOLATE
MIXING BOWL MUD CAKE

SERVES 8–10

Too often when I have a chocolate cake, I just think: why isn't this a brownie? Chocolate cakes are rarely dense, chocolatey and indulgent enough for my tastes. This recipe is a corrective, combining a moist, rich cake with gooey chocolate custard and luscious ganache. Better than brownies? It just might be!

A

1 egg yolk

2 tablespoons cornflour (cornstarch)

50 g (1¾ oz/scant ½ cup) caster (superfine) sugar

200 ml (7 fl oz/scant 1 cup) whole milk

3 tablespoons double (heavy) cream

6 tablespoons cocoa powder

Whisk together the egg yolk, cornflour, and sugar in a medium bowl; it will form a rough, crumbly mass. Whisk in a splash of milk to make a thin paste, then the rest of it, little by little, until smooth. Stir in the cream and cocoa powder, then cook, uncovered, for 3 minutes 30 seconds–4 minutes, whisking well after each minute, until very thick. Chill in the refrigerator with a piece of cling film (plastic wrap) or parchment placed directly on the surface of the custard.

B

200 g (7 oz) butter

250 g (9 oz/1⅓ cup) light brown sugar

3 eggs

200 g (7 oz/1⅔ cups) plain (all-purpose) flour

70 g (2½ oz) cocoa powder

2 teaspoons bicarbonate of soda (baking soda)

1 teaspoon baking powder

1 teaspoon salt

150 ml (5 fl oz/scant ⅔ cup) milk

4 tablespoons yoghurt

1 tablespoon vanilla extract

For best results, have everything at room temperature before you begin. Place the butter in a large plastic bowl and cook, uncovered, for 1 minute on power level 5 so it becomes very soft (it's okay if it melts a bit). Tip in the sugar and whisk hard for a few minutes until the mixture is relatively light and smooth. Beat in the eggs, one at a time, until well mixed. Tip in the flour, cocoa powder, bicarbonate of soda, baking powder and salt. Mix with a spatula, scraping down the sides and the bottom as you go until a smooth batter forms, then stir in the milk, yoghurt and vanilla and mix well. Scrape down the sides of the bowl once again so you have relatively clean sides and a tidy pile of batter at the bottom. Cover and cook for 12–14 minutes, until a thin skewer or toothpick inserted into the middle comes out clean. Leave to cool for a while, then tip out, upside-down, onto a plate, to cool completely.

100 g (3½ oz) milk chocolate, finely chopped

100 g (3½ oz) dark chocolate, finely chopped

100 ml (3½ fl oz/scant ½ cup) double (heavy) cream

Place the chopped chocolates in a bowl and the double cream in a separate bowl or jug. Cook the cream for about 1 minute until steaming (but ideally not boiling). Pour the hot cream over the chocolate and leave for a minute, then mix it all together with a spatula so the chocolate melts evenly through the cream. If there are any stubborn unmelted chunks of chocolate, microwave for another 10–15 seconds and stir again until the ganache is totally smooth.

To serve, cut the cooled cake in half through the middle to make two layers. The bottom layer will be wider than the top, so cut off the outer edge of this layer so each one has roughly the same diameter. Crumble the trimmings into the cocoa custard (A) and mix well, then spread the custard on top of the bottom layer. Lay the top layer back on the cake, then pour over the ganache (B) while it's still warm. Chill in the refrigerator to set before slicing and serving.

BOURBON MAPLE PEACH COOKIE CRUMBLE THING

SERVES 8–10

I tried to make a crumble in the microwave. It was delicious, but it wasn't really a crumble – the topping was soft, moist and buttery, more like a flapjack or an oatmeal cookie than a crumble. I decided this is no bad thing, no bad thing at all. Here is the recipe.

A

50 g (1¾ oz) oats (any kind except pinhead or steel-cut)

25 g (1 oz) pumpkin seeds

25 g (1 oz) almonds

Stir together the oats, pumpkin seeds and almonds in a 23 cm (9 in) ceramic baking dish and cook, uncovered, in 1-minute intervals, stirring after each interval until the mixture smells nutty and aromatic. For me this took 4 minutes. Tip the mixture out into a bowl and leave to cool for a few minutes.

B

60 g (2 oz/½ cup) plain (all-purpose) flour

40 g (1½ oz/¼ cup) brown sugar (any kind)

1 teaspoon ground cinnamon

a pinch or two of salt

100 g (3½ oz) butter, cubed

Add the flour, sugar, cinnamon and salt to the oat mixture (A) and stir to combine. Smash in the butter until it forms a sticky cookie dough-like consistency; the warmth of the oats may melt the butter slightly, which is fine and good.

C

1 tin (250 g/9 oz drained weight) of sliced peaches

150 g (5½ oz) frozen berries (I used half cherries and half blueberries and both were lovely)

1 tablespoon maple syrup

2 tablespoons bourbon or Irish whiskey

½ teaspoon vanilla extract

any creamy accompaniment you like – vanilla ice cream, double (heavy) cream, custard, sour cream, mascarpone or Greek yoghurt

Ensure the peaches are very well drained; use a sieve (fine mesh strainer) for this. Combine the drained peaches, frozen berries and maple syrup in the baking dish and stir. Cook, uncovered, for 7 minutes. Stir in the bourbon and vanilla, then top with the oatmeal cookie mixture (B). Cook for another 8 minutes, uncovered, then leave to stand for 5 minutes before serving. Serve with the creamy topping of your choice.

FIGS POACHED IN CARDAMOM SYRUP WITH FRESH CHEESE

SERVES 4–6

Over the past year or so I have had the enormous privilege of sitting in on a migrant men's support group called Giants, part of the migrant and refugee charity Praxis. Members of the group have been regularly cooking lunch for each other, sharing their recipes and stories in the process, working towards the publication of their own cookbook. One of the group members (who also happens to work for Praxis) shared his incredible story of coming of age as a young communist in Colombia, surrounded by political violence and guerrilla warfare, and how he eventually came to settle in the UK. He also served one of the most delicious things I've eaten in recent memory, *dulce de brevas con queso fresco*: plump figs, preserved and semi-candied in a thick sugar syrup, served with a hard, salty, fresh cheese (which he made from scratch himself). This is inspired by that dessert – it's not as good as his, of course, and the use of cardamom and a different kind of cheese makes it not even that similar – but nevertheless, I'll think of him and his story every time I eat it.

5 cardamom pods

100 g (3½ oz/scant ½ cup) caster (superfine) sugar

100 ml (3½ fl oz/scant ½ cup) water

50 g (1¾ oz/2 tablespoons) honey

6 small fresh figs (about 150 g/5½ oz)

6 dried figs (about 100 g/3½ oz)

Crush the cardamom pods with something hard (I used the jar they came in) so they split open and the seeds inside are bruised. Place these in a medium bowl along with the sugar, water and honey. Cook, uncovered, for 2 minutes. Trim the hard stems off of the figs, then score a cross in the bottom of each fresh one. Place all of fresh and dried figs in the syrup (they will float – not a problem) and cook for 4 minutes. Leave the figs to chill completely in the refrigerator. (You can have them warm, but for me they aren't as tasty.)

100–120 g (3½–4¼ oz) salty, hard cheese, such as Wensleydale, ricotta salata or Manchego, sliced into 4–6 pieces

Remove the figs from the syrup (A) and place in small dishes. Serve with slices of cheese and some of the syrup drizzled over.

PBJ CROISSANT PUDDING

SERVES 4

Due to some weird glitch in my online shopping, or perhaps due to some weird glitch in my thumb (or my brain), I recently wound up with five packs of four croissants. Twenty croissants! I didn't even want four croissants; they were just part of some multi-buy deal. We all ate croissants for a couple days, and I gave some to the neighbours, and there were still too many croissants. What to do? Make croissant bread pudding, of course. I have always wanted to try this, and I was frankly amazed at how easy (and delicious) it was in the microwave.

1 egg

5 tablespoons double (heavy) cream

5 tablespoons milk

1 teaspoon vanilla extract

4 stale croissants, torn up

4 heaped tablespoons peanut butter

4 heaped tablespoons jam (any will do, but I used this as an opportunity to clear out the nearly empty jars in my refrigerator, which included grape, marmalade and chuckleberry)

Demerara sugar, to taste

In a circular 18–3 cm (7–9 in) baking dish, beat together the egg, cream, milk and vanilla until smooth. Tip in the croissants, peanut butter and jam, and toss – don't stir too much, because there should still be globs of un-mixed peanut butter and jam throughout. Press the croissants down into the dish, then leave to soak for at least 30 minutes, or up to overnight. Cook, uncovered, for 6 minutes. Sprinkle over some Demerara sugar, then leave to cool and set for at least 5 minutes before serving. This is nice hot, but also delicious cold.

ABOUT THE AUTHOR

Tim Anderson is a chef and author who specialises in Japanese and American food. Since winning *MasterChef* in 2011, he has written seven books on Japanese cookery, including *Ramen Forever*, *Your Home Izakaya* and the *JapanEasy* series. He currently lives in South London with his wife Laura, daughter Tig, son Felix and FIV-positive cat Baloo.

ACKNOWLEDGEMENTS

I am grateful to have had the support of such a wonderful team as I venture into the uncharted waters of non-Japanese recipe writing. On the editorial side at Hardie Grant, I have to thank Kajal Mistry and Eila Purvis for having the confidence to let me try something new, and Esme Curtis for her precise and sympathetic editing. I owe a big thanks to Ruth Tewkesbury and all of the PR, sales and marketing teams at HG as well, for fully getting behind this weird little book.

It was a joy to shoot this with the dream team of Sam Harris, Beca Jones, Tamara Vos and Rachel Vere. As much as I love microwave cooking, I do not tend to think of it as photogenic, but I have been blown away with the shots in this book. Well done team!

Thanks also to Evi O and her studio for yet another striking design! Can't wait to see what you come up with for *Hokkaido*.

And finally, thanks to Holly Arnold for making all of this happen, and to my family, for eating almost nothing but microwaved food every day for months while I worked on these recipes!